Christianity According to The Christ

Walter Justice

Christianity According to the Christ

ISBN 978-0-9765764-4-0

Dedicated to Alla, the most precious of all gems…a daughter of the truth.

Table of Contents

Prologue

"A person often meets his destiny on the road he took to avoid it."

JEAN DE LA FONTAINE

After studying philosophy and wrestling with the 'big questions,' I attended seminary and learned biblical theology. I found both endeavors worthwhile. More than anything else, however, I wanted to serve God and others. I possessed tremendous zeal and threw myself into church and community work. My ministry involved preaching, networking with like-minded leaders, seasons of extended prayer and fasting, and implementing citywide transformation strategies. Oh, how wrong I was…

My Father halted my misguided, but good intentions. He was more concerned about my heart than nameless and faceless multitudes. Thankfully, my career ended as quickly as it began. The religious system I campaigned for, and wholeheartedly participated in was just as wicked, if not more so, than all the community strongholds put together. Evil hid behind the cross.

Today, I cherish my intimate relationships. God is my best Friend. I walk with Him in the cool of the day, and we share our hearts with each other. I spend more time listening than speaking. God tells me the most amazing things. I cannot live without my best Friend.

Recently, in a dream, the Lord asked me to do something for Him.

DREAM:

There I stood in a valley. Three underground tunnels extended off into the distance. I could easily follow each tunnel's path because the topsoil was raised and cracked. A voice behind me said, "You can't stray an inch." I knew the voice was asking me to go underground and tunnel like the others, whoever they were. I stood paralyzed, terrified. How was I supposed to know where to go, let alone not stray an inch? I also realized I wouldn't be able to see my path while tunneling. The challenge felt insurmountable.

In the next frame, I'm still standing in the valley, but now in front of a huge hacienda style home. The home was one story, flat, with a red tiled roof and covered several acres of land. The grounds were well kept, nearly immaculate.

I then found myself floating in the sky facing three buildings that progressively descended down a jagged mountain cliff. The tallest building was wooden, multistoried and overtly ornate. It resembled a European cathedral. Sharp gothic steeples protruded everywhere. Balconies jetted out at each level. The lofty structure possessed only a couple of tiny

portholes and no windows.

The next building was slightly lower. It too was wooden and multi-storied, but lacked the hard, vertical lines and intricate details of the previous structure. The building looked like an enormous mansion, and, instead of balconies, possessed a number of windows of various sizes.

The last and lowest building was ultra-modern and composed entirely of steel and glass. Steel girders anchored the structure while glass walls made it feel accessible. There were three stair-stacked levels. Tremendous engineering went into this symmetrical building.

The final scene placed me in the ultra-modern building. A man dressed in black, high-tech body armor quickly and authoritatively approached me. He held a short-barreled assault weapon in his right hand. The soldier raised, pointed and shot his weapon at me. I thought to myself, 'I'm going to die.' Milky white liquid shot out and hit me in the chest. I looked down, saw the liquid bounce off of me and form a small puddle on the ground. I quickly became aware that I too held an assault weapon and fired back. My gun also sprayed white liquid. I hit the soldier in the torso propelling him across the room and onto his back. Immediately, two more soldiers appeared and opened fire. Once again, the white liquid struck me, and it fell to the ground. I returned fire, and like their associate, they both went flying. End of dream.

INTERPRETATION:

The tunnels represent underground ministry. By its very nature, underground ministry is dirty and dangerous work, and receives little if any earthly rewards. Jesus was an underground minister, and therefore, underground ministry is the highest calling in the kingdom of God. As the three tunnels indicate, only a few accept this high calling. The underground serves the unseen: thieves, gangsters, the diseased, prostitutes, the forgotten, perverts, addicts, the poor, failures, the unlovely, youngsters, the old, and widows-- all those found on the periphery of society. These individuals are the precious ones Institutional Christianity has rejected and banished.

Underground ministry is a journey of faith. Since the underground minister is submerged, or underground, he or she cannot see where to go. And so, the underground must be Spirit led, otherwise, disaster lies imminent. As the prophet Isaiah said, *"Whether you turn to the right or to the left, your ears will hear a voice behind you, saying, this is the way; walk in it."* **[Isaiah 30:21]**

Each building represented an epoch of Christianity. The first house, the one-storied hacienda, was indicative of the early church. There were no hierarchies, only familial relationships. Their intimacy advanced health and order as evidenced by the manicured grounds.

The hacienda was located in a valley. Rather than exult themselves, the early church lived in humility. The red tiled roof signified the blood of the Lord Jesus Christ that covered their entire lives. Additionally, most food is grown in valleys. The early church fed on scripture.

The gothic, wooden cathedral represented the Dark Ages. Wood burns and is therefore symbolic of the earthly and temporal. Beautiful, ornate exteriors readily masked evil interiors. The lack of windows prevented the light of the Gospel from shining inside and dispelling darkness. The cathedral's lofty mountain position and tall steeples allude to pride. The balconies denote levels of corruption; the dishonest exalt themselves and desire to be seen. From heaven's perspective, the Dark Ages were, perhaps, the low point in church history.

The third building, the mountain mansion, corresponds to the Reformation. The steeples and balconies were noticeably absent, and with them, the extreme arrogance and corruption indicative of the previous epoch. The structure's smoother lines indicated a change of heart. The multitude of windows demonstrates truth and life reentering the church. However, this building was also wooden, and so, earthen. The Reformation eradicated a number of excesses, but failed to usher in genuine transformation. The Dark Ages and the Reformation were similar, yet different.

The fourth and final building symbolizes the modern church. Glass and steel are manufactured, man-made. The modern church is contrived. Nevertheless, the abundant use of glass allowed the return of minor truths: evangelism, healing, prophecy, deliverance, worship, and prayer. A layered design suggests hierarchies still exist, but streamlined: pastor, associate pastor, and worship leader. Symmetry speaks of human ingenuity and efficiency. In other words, what works? Since this building was designed, and therefore blueprinted, duplicates can be constructed and franchised. The building was accessible, yet cold and unauthentic.

The soldiers stand for professional clergy. These professionals are trend chasers and incorporate the latest fads and technologies into their respective kingdoms. The clergy police others by spraying them with the pure milk of the word. However, since the soldiers misuse God's word, they are powerless. But, when Spirit directed, the word of God is powerful. **[Hebrews 4:12]**

A fight is brewing.

God calls each and every person. Whether one responds is his or her prerogative. The Lord's plans and purposes are divine, and as such, humanly impossible to comprehend. If chosen ones aren't overwhelmed, then they've probably failed to grasp their calling. Only through the empowerment of the Spirit do chosen ones step into the purposes and plans of God, moment-by-moment and day-by-day. The details are just as important as the overall scheme of things. The majority of believers rarely fulfill the purposes of God because they quit somewhere along the way by refusing new challenges and change. The journey requires patience and endurance, and most of all, great courage.

I'm overwhelmed, and at times, even a little intimidated. That's honest. I refuse to parrot, *"but God has not given us a spirit of fear, but of power, of love, and a sound mind."* **[2 Timothy 1:7]** Parrots are fearful people. Hollow, positive confession attempts to bolster faint-heartedness. The best thing anyone can do is honestly face oneself and keep it real. No one is fooled, especially God. The biggest lies we tell are to ourselves.

My heart's desire is to be Christ-like. I lost my life by embracing Jesus as Lord and Savior. Jesus went underground, and so have I. As my dream revealed, others are tunneling, and have been doing so for some time. We are never alone, nor does eternity rest solely upon our shoulders. Inspiration originates with the Holy Spirit, and God graciously allows believers to participate in His divine purposes.

I continue to spend time with my best Friend, rather than running to ghettos, searching for broken souls, or chasing invalids.

Interestingly, the underground finds me. Tunneling is an attitude or a condition of the heart, and not laborious action. People are naturally drawn to Jesus.

As I stated earlier, the Lord tells me the most amazing things. I will be sharing a number of His secrets in the following pages. Everything in this book centers on Jesus. My Lord, or the Christ, polarizes people; some experience comfort, and others take offense. For those weary and unacknowledged souls who travel along the highways and byways with Jesus, this book affirms and will prove therapeutic.

Indictments

"I know that most men—not only those considered clever, but even those who are very clever and capable of understanding most difficult scientific, mathematical, or philosophic, problems—can seldom discern even the simplest and most obvious truth if it be such as obliges them to admit the falsity of conclusions they have formed, perhaps with much difficulty—conclusions of which they are proud, which they have taught to others, and on which they have built their lives."

LEO NIKOLAEVICH TOLSTOI

I am a full-blown heretic...sort of. I exited mainstream Christianity a long time ago. However, I'm not your every day, run-of-the-mill heretic. In the past, a few folks stereotyped me as a fundamentalist. That's baffling. I've had friends who were murderers, addicts, whores, thugs, homosexuals, and just like everyone else, I struggled at times too. I never once told them to turn or burn. On the contrary, I loved them, and found myself interceding regularly on their behalf, and continue to do so. I remind myself of Jesus' scathing charge against the Pharisees:

"…I tell you the truth, the tax collectors and the prostitutes are entering the kingdom of God ahead of you." **[Matthew 21:31]**

I no longer fix folks. Although it's taken me years to figure out, I've finally realized that fixing people is the sole responsibility of

God, and God alone. When I undertook a human project, almost without exception I failed, and in general harmed instead of healing. The human heart is God's domain. He's still transforming mine.

My close friends consider me a Bible-head. This characterization fits much better. I believe the Bible is the infallible word of God, and the final authority regarding Christian doctrine. I believe Jesus was and is the incarnate representation of God. I believe He died on the cross for all of creation, rose on the third day, ascended to heaven and is seated at the right hand of the Father. God sent His Spirit to reside in the hearts of all who call Jesus Lord and Savior. Pretty orthodox, eh? I'm an orthodox heretic.

Early on, those who departed from Roman Catholic dogma were branded as heretics, and quite often, the cost was extremely severe, even resulting in death. Later, a whole movement of dissension rose up known as The Reformation. Like their former taskmasters, the Reformers persecuted nonconformists too; countless Anabaptists and Jews were tortured and killed. Both the Roman Catholics and the Reformers viewed themselves as true disciples of the Lord Jesus Christ. Whatever happened to the commandment of love thy neighbor as thyself? **[Matthew 19:19]** Clever theologians undoubtedly misconstrued the notion. Yet, if one reads the Gospels, and specifically The Parable of the Good Samaritan, Jesus leaves us without excuse. Children as young as three and four years old can easily recognize the good neighbor in the story. **[Luke 10:25-37]** Thus far, nobody has flogged me, nor attempted to burn me--thank God. I've been called nasty names though. According to my Lord, however, I should rejoice, and do. **[Luke 6:22-23]**

My heresy emerges from orthodoxy. I have four pressing indictments against Institutional Christianity.

INDICTMENT #1: *Christians don't follow Jesus, the Christ.*

Jesus' unique claim,

"I am the way and the truth and the life. No one comes to the Father except through me." **[John 14:6]**

Jesus is the Way. Nobody comes into the presence of the Father except through the Person of the Lord Jesus Christ. As the Gate, the Lord determines who enters and who doesn't. **[John 10:7]** The Way is difficult and narrow, and few find Him. **[Matthew 7:14]**

Jesus is also the Truth, or the Son of God. He did not take on human form merely to abolish cosmic evil, or spare humanity from the wrath of an angry old tyrant. The Lord lived, died and was resurrected in order to restore fellowship and intimacy between Himself and His beloved.

By pursuing the Way, and embracing the Truth, one enters the Life. Jesus, the Lover of our souls, freed captives from the devil's dominion and the power of sin. **[John 8:34-37]** The believer's new life is an unconditional, eternal, intimate relationship with the Father of all creation. **[John 10:10]** The beloved lives in God, and God lives in the beloved. **[John 15:1-17]**

Then--Why does Institutional Christianity place a premium on the Pauline Epistles, or other biblical texts, including the Old Testament, while relegating the life and teachings of Jesus secondary status? Are they followers of Jesus or not? Does leadership ignorantly presume the greatest mysteries of the Lord Jesus Christ have already been discovered? Or, are they followers of Paul or Peter, or perhaps Abraham?

All scripture derives from the breath of God. However, one's foundation determines his or her awareness. Only through the lens of the Lord Jesus Christ is scripture revealed. He is the divine Key to understanding the Bible. Nevertheless, professional clergy validate worldly ideologies by handpicking passages, twisting the Gospel, and developing self-serving doctrines. I listen to the madness virtually every day, and I'm sickened. In turn, Joe and Suzy Christian never realize the Life. Most parishioners don't even know Jesus. Paul said,

"For I resolved to know nothing while I was with you except Jesus Christ and him crucified." **[1 Corinthians 2:2]**

And Jesus said of Himself,

"...Anyone who has seen me has seen the Father..." **[John 14:9]**

Institutional Christianity must return to the simplicity of the Gospel. If one builds their faith upon anyone or anything other than the Lord Jesus Christ, he or she will fail. **[Luke 6:46-49]** He is the Cornerstone on which all-else stands. **[Mark 12:10]** If believers begin with Jesus, they will finish with Him. **[Revelation 1:8]**

INDICTMENT #2: *Christians don't love.*

Since Institutional Christianity departed from the true Foundation, hardness of heart ensued. Jesus confronted the Pharisees regarding this very issue:

...You diligently study the Scriptures because you think that by them you possess eternal life. These are the scriptures that testify about me, yet you refuse to come to me to have life. I do not accept praise from men, but I know you. I know that you do not have the love of God in your hearts. I have come in my Father's name, and you do not accept me; but if someone else comes in his own name, you will accept him. How can you believe if you accept praise from one another, yet make no effort to obtain the praise that comes from only God.
[John 5:39-44]

These professionals were power brokers and the most learned men of their day. They knew scripture frontwards and backwards, and could quote verbatim any Old Testament text. Yet, for all their learning they failed to recognize the Messiah. The Pharisees established doctrines that reinforced their position and rule and enslaved the people. Those who possessed notoriety or title were immediately honored and respected.

Evil is cyclical and repeats itself throughout history. Paul, like his Lord and Savior, confronted hardness of heart. **2 Timothy 3:1-9** says:

But mark this: There will be terrible times in the last days. People will be lovers of themselves, lovers of money, boastful, proud, abusive, disobedient to their parents, ungrateful, unholy, without self-control, brutal, no lovers of the good, treacherous, rash, conceited, lovers of pleasure rather than lovers of God--having a form of godliness but denying its power. Have nothing to do with them. They are the kind who worm their way into homes and gain control over weak-willed women, who are loaded down with sins and are swayed by all kinds of evil desires, always learning but never able to acknowledge the truth. Just as Jannes and Jambres opposed Moses, so also these men oppose the truth--men of depraved minds, who as far as the faith is concerned, are rejected. But they will not get very far because, as in the case of those men, their folly will be clear to everyone.

A tenet of Charismania is immediately exposed, *"having a form of godliness but denying its power."* Within this passage, power makes no allusion to signs and wonders. Rather, this passage indicates the powerless razzle-dazzle like Pharaoh's court magicians Jannes and Jambres. Wizards use tricks. God's faithful operate in love as evidenced by the fruit of the Spirit. Jesus emphasized fruit, and not miracles. **[Matthew 7:15-20]**

Paul used a phrase reminiscent of Jesus, *"always learning but never able to acknowledge the Truth."* (Emphasis mine) Jesus said in the previous passage, *"You diligently study the Scriptures because you think by them you possess eternal life. These are the Scriptures that testify about me, yet you refuse to come to me to have life."* Hauntingly familiar, isn't it?

Institutional Christianity possesses enough resources to fill virtually every university library. Unsaved Christians are always learning but never able to acknowledge the Truth--the Lord Jesus Christ.

Hardness of heart fosters endless learning and spiritual busyness. Knowledge instills pride and puffs up without God. **[1 Corinthians 8:1]** One must validate him or herself. Knowledge soothes inferiority by covering personal inadequacies. Insecure people employ trivia and minor truths to create a sense of superiority, and shore up their low self-esteem.

The other crutch is spiritual busyness. Institutional Christianity demands effort, and effort determines what is good enough. Religious people work for their salvation. Fear generates busyness. Once again, the godless rely on themselves.

Conversely, God is love, and His presence vanquishes fear. **[1 John 4:16-19]** The Spirit of God resides in true Christians. **[Romans 8:9]** Believers place a premium on relationships and rejoice in the accomplishments of others. Self-worth is determined by God rather than works. Peace, calmness and confidence rule because there is no fear in love. The beloved belong to Jesus, and Jesus belongs to the Father. **[John 15:9-14]**

INDICTMENT #3: *Christians employ self-serving doctrines.*

Institutional Christianity's wrong approach has led further and further from the Christ. Years ago, long before GPS units, I travelled in the Florida Everglades with a friend. We became disoriented and took a wrong turn. The two-lane road was well maintained and used. We realized something wasn't right after driving fifty or sixty miles. There were no overpasses or intersections, just miles and miles of green. We turned around and drove back to our departure point. Then and only then did we begin traveling toward our destination.

Sincerity does not guarantee truth. Just because Institutional Christianity zealously defends her doctrines and rituals does not necessitate correctness. Many of those doctrines sound holy, but incite arrogance. Other tenets torment and enslave. Does Institutional Christianity look like Jesus, or the government of the United States, or a major corporation? As Institutional Christianity pursues respectability and temporal praise, she continues distancing herself from the Christ.

Organized religion mimics secular institutions by exercising control over others. Conversely, Jesus represented heaven. His entire ministry confronted worldly powers, then and now. He served instead of controlling, and gave instead of taxing. Jesus' rule resembled a close-knit, intimate family, and not a top-down, hierarchical regime. Either Jesus is Lord or He's not. If believers are submitted to Jesus, then they demonstrate His values. Otherwise, folks are unknowingly representing a false god.

Jesus rebuked the Ephesian Church for leaving their first love. **[Revelation 2:4]** He went on to say, *"Remember the height from which you have fallen! Repent and do the things you did at first. If you do not repent, I will come and remove your lampstand from its place."* **[Revelation 2:5]** His warning remains timeless.

INDICTMENT #4: *Christians suffer from 'causefusion.'*

When the Romans conquered ancient Israel and the Middle East, they encountered swamps, and their soldiers became ill and died. After draining the swamps, the disease subsided too. The Romans incorrectly believed swamp air caused their sickness. Mala means bad, and aria means air. The Latin name for the disease, malaria, remains to this day.

Modern science now knows mosquitoes carry parasites and inject microscopic killers into victims. Swamps are breeding grounds, but not the actual cause of malaria.

Although the Romans indirectly addressed the problem, and approached the truth, they were nevertheless wrong. The Romans lived in a state of 'causefusion.' **[Shore 32]**

Institutional Christianity suffers from causefusion too. Since most parishioners don't know Jesus, they can't fellowship with the Father. Without intimate knowledge, the godless are forced to derive their understanding of God from popular opinion, construed scripture, hearsay, fabricated stories, and even accusations. In turn, religion has created a mean, hateful destroyer. Or, he's a slave driver who tallies every evil action and thought, and joyfully punishes transgressors. These people worship the devil. Their pastors are messengers of fear and darkness. Others pray to a doting candy man hoping money rains down on them. This is also the devil. **[Luke 16:13]** Here, silver-tongued dandies water greedy hearts.

Like the Romans and malaria, the issue becomes especially menacing the closer one approximates to the truth, yet remains misinformed. One does the right thing for the wrong reason. For example, a person prays for and ministers to others. However, rather than being motivated by the love of Christ, he seeks personal significance and recognition. Or, perhaps someone volunteers at a women's shelter. Instead of simply serving the downtrodden, she attempts to work her way into Heaven. These deceived souls serve a god, but not the Lord Jesus Christ.

Institutional Christians will undoubtedly charge me with arrogance: 'Why are you the only one who has the Truth?' or 'You can't judge my heart!' or 'I have my own beliefs.' Jesus is no respecter of persons. **[James 2:1]** I need tremendous grace and mercy in my pilgrimage. However, I know Jesus, and what passes for Christianity, is not--not even close. Like the chorus from the children's Sunday school song, "the Bible tells me so."

Others accuse me of being angry and bitter, and as of late, cynical. I demonstrated those traits during a number of seasons in my life, and sad to say, worse. I've been flat out mean, hateful and rebellious. These days, though, I don't think those charges fit. Disturbed? Yes. Disgusted? Without question.

Those who accuse me of anger and bitterness often use their accusations as life rafts; when their beliefs become untenable, they jump ship, and float away saying, "You're just angry." or "You're bitter." I'm just the opposite; I'm grateful. I would never know my Father the way I do without my struggles, and His loving discipline. My failures made me who I am.

Alternative thoughts are unsettling, especially if one has held contrary views, and even campaigned for those views. Alternative thoughts often feel counterintuitive. I live in the Northwest, and for a few years, in Canada. The roads get icy each winter. If one hits an icy patch while driving, the worst thing she can do is slam on her brakes. The vehicle immediately slides, and almost without exception, crashes. And yet, from firsthand experience, I know this is exactly what one feels like doing. It's natural. Ease off the gas, and drive straight through. Do the same thing when challenged! Don't slam on your brakes by throwing your hands up in the air and exclaiming, 'No!' Rather, ease off your convictions, listen, and go forward. A person develops a deeper understanding whether she agrees or not. And, you may completely disagree. That's OK too.

A long time ago I heard the term 'pink elephant.' At first, I had no idea what this term meant. I automatically associated it with bad drugs or a crazy drunken stupor. This is in fact one of pink elephant's meanings; a person is so inebriated that he sees pink elephants. There's another meaning though, and in a way, much more provocative and insightful. We've all been with a group of friends where everyone wants to talk about an issue, but, because the subject matter is so volatile, folks avoid it. Or, metaphorically speaking, there's a huge pink elephant in the room, and everyone walks around, crawls under, or climbs over the gigantic beast, and yet, all are unwilling to acknowledge the presence of the pastel monster.

Pink elephants are one thing, and sacred cows another. Sacred cows are smaller, and not nearly as colorful, but these idols are every bit the obstacle, if not more so. Since these cows are sacred, you better not touch them. I understand the meaning firsthand. I visited Nepal years ago. Sacred cows roamed the streets. If someone harassed one of these animals, he or she went to prison. If a driver inadvertently struck and killed a sacred cow with their vehicle, he or she received a death sentence. Strangely enough, back then and perhaps still today, if a person was accidentally struck and killed, the driver received a twenty-year prison term.

Again, I'm an orthodox heretic. I no longer live under the law, but above it, dwelling in the realm of unmerited grace. My spiritual condition makes me an outlaw. From my vantage point, I watch slaves worship the sacred cows of religion. This book hunts sacred cows. If you're faint of heart give this read to someone else. If you enter the hunt, you will be confronted, challenged, and perhaps, even shown your error. Successful hunts are bloody. The older and more revered the beast, the messier the kill. Scary? Few people possess the fortitude to say, 'I was wrong.' For those who can, incredible liberty and freedom awaits them.

Before the hunt begins, however, proper preparations are required. And so, in the next chapter, I establish the importance of love in relation to thought. I then present a Biblical account of who God really is. I also take a second look at Jezebel and the antichrist spirit in chapter four. Thereafter, I hunt and hopefully dispel the idolatry supporting the sacred cows of money, power, success, spiritual warfare and prayer, and lastly, inner healing and forgiveness.

An epilogue closes this book.

Knowing and Understanding Through Love

"The only source of knowledge is experience."
ALBERT EINSTEIN

The West is inundated with facts. Information once confined to a privileged few is now readily available to all. The Internet is a seemingly an unlimited resource. One can obtain everything from personal background checks to detailed scientific dissertations online. Computers and smart-phones enable folks to surf the Internet, download music, read e-books, and even film historic events. Technology generated unrestricted information.

The reality of unrestricted information applies directly to Christendom as well. Multivolume commentaries are stored on tiny flash drives. Any Christian can research obscure, ancient works or specific historical events via electronic study aids. Clergy are no longer the sole disseminators of religious facts. Only choice and desire separate the learned from the unlearned.

Regardless of the field of study, however, information does not beget knowledge, or knowledge understanding. Other factors bear consideration as well.

In this chapter, I discuss how love pertains to knowledge, meaning, interpretation and understanding. Each concept is examined in relation to God and scripture. The Bible is quite clear,

"The fear of the Lord is the beginning of wisdom, and knowledge of the Holy One understanding." **[Proverbs 9:10]**

KNOWLEDGE

I remember reading about a young woman who hated the smell of roses. She first encountered the scent during the funeral of her mother. The initial experience seared her soul. Thereafter, she always associated roses with death. **[Herz 39]**

Another woman adored pungent skunk. She fondly recalled a country drive as a child with her mother. The rural setting lent itself to skunks, and with them, their infamous odor. Consequently, the young woman linked skunks to warm memories, and found the scent pleasant. **[Herz ix]**

Personal experience enhances or poisons knowledge. Most people like roses. Yet, because of one woman's experience, she didn't. Could she recognize and identify roses? Yes. Although she obviously knew what a rose was, her past experience poisoned her knowledge. Roses are good: the plant possesses aesthetic value, is rich in vitamins, and suitable for human consumption.

The young woman represents a large segment of humanity. For example, some folks hated school, and dropped out. Even so, many people, including dropouts, readily endorse education. The vast majority of dropouts lived through difficult circumstances during their early years.

Similarly, others are stuck in a time warp. The former homecoming queen or star quarterback slides into obscurity. They view their lives as lackluster because everything pales in comparison to their glory days.

Multitudes turned to Institutional Christianity for spiritual guidance and understanding. Yet, if Institutional Christianity misrepresented God, and construed scripture, then it stands to reason most folks were spiritually misguided and eventually disillusioned. As a result, few possess a healthy knowledge of God or scripture.

An immediate family member of mine grew up in Christian legalism. Ministers preached 'at' the congregation, instead of 'to' the congregation. Sermons highlighted sin. Trespassers were brought before the entire church, and shamed. Holier-than-thou leaders stressed 'don't', and whipped sheep with scripture. My family member came to believe from toxic personal experience that God was mean, strict, and worst of all, punitive. Thankfully, the Lord Jesus Christ divinely revealed Himself to her, and she now experiences intense, vibrant intimacy with God.

FAITH, HOPE, AND LOVE

Faith, hope and love are critical to any field of knowledge or relationship. **[1 Corinthians 13:13]** Without the big three, especially love, knowledge stagnates and eventually fizzles. As love matures knowledge increases.

I remember itinerant ministers blowing through my hometown years ago and testifying to supernatural exploits that seemingly rivaled the book of Acts. During that same season, however, my spiritual life could best be characterized as tame and ordinary. Most folks embellish, and more than likely, a few of these ministers did too. And still, my heart burned.

I also recalled a number of biblical heroes: Abraham gave his wife away, but remained God's friend **[Genesis 20, Isaiah 41:8]**; Moses murdered, but spoke face to Face with God **[Exodus 2:12, 33:11]**; Rahab was a prostitute, but saved her entire family **[Joshua 2]**; Caleb was born into slavery, but routed giants **[Numbers 13:6, Joshua 15:14]**; Samson womanized, but overpowered a nation **[Judges 14-16]**; David murdered and fornicated, but had a heart like God's **[2 Samuel 11, 1 Samuel 13:13-14]**; Elijah suffered depression, but flew to heaven in a fiery chariot **[1 Kings 19:3-5, 2 Kings 2:13]**; Jeremiah feared for his life, but prophesied to nations **[Jeremiah 20:7-18, 1:5]**; Peter denied Christ, but helped establish the church **[Matthew 26:69-75, Acts 2:17-41]**; Paul destroyed families, but penned the majority of the New Testament. **[Acts 9:1-2, Romans, 1 &2 Corinthians, Galatians, Ephesians, Philippians, Colossians, 1 & 2 Thessalonians, 1 & 2 Timothy, Titus, and Philemon]** All flawed and all great.

As I reflected, and considered all these things, my heart welled up. There had to be more! My present reality was unacceptable. What made these ministers or Bible greats better than me, or others for that matter? Why couldn't I experience a supernatural life? Soon, I believed I could, and that conviction refused to go away. And, this is the essence of hope: A belief or conviction that rejects circumstances and remains unshakeable.

Most folks lose heart far too soon. A bad class destroys an entire school year. A hurtful break-up sours future relationships. Someone gets benched and quits a sport. Pious, cliquey Christians belittle spiritual quests.

Conversely, hope transcends difficult obstacles. A bad class exemplifies great classes. A failed relationship means Mr. Right is closer. Getting benched involves practicing one's favorite sport all the more. Pious, cliquey Christians ignite believers past mediocrity.

Jesus came across a Samaritan woman on one of His many journeys. **[John 4:4-42]** He supernaturally spoke into her life. **[Vs. 16-17]** The Samaritan woman returned to her town and told others about Jesus. **[Vs. 29]** The Samaritans, like the Jews, waited or hoped for the Messiah. **[Vs. 25]** With hope burning in their hearts, other Samaritans went out to see Jesus, and believed. **[Vs. 30 & 42]** An entire community found God.

FAITH

Over the years, I've heard several definitions of faith. Someone once said, "Faith is risk." Another said, "Faith is trust." Others quote **Hebrews 11:1**, *"Now faith is being sure of what we hope for and certain of what we do not see."* But, what does that mean? What is the essence of faith, and is it integral to knowledge?

Christians make faith out to be spooky and ethereal. Intellectuals scoff at faith, and consider those who hold fast to spiritual fidelity as weak and simple minded. Nothing could be further from the truth.

Humankind is made in the image and likeness of God. **[Genesis 1:26]** God is faithful. **[2 Corinthians 1:18]** In turn, people are innately fashioned for fidelity. This is why scripture says without faith it is impossible to please God. **[Hebrews 11:6]**

So, does everyone possess faith, or only Christians? Everyone does. Again, people are spiritually wired for fidelity. Remember the Bible's definition of faith, *"being sure of we hope for and certain of what we do not see"*. A businessperson believes in success and sets out to amassing wealth. A researcher believes in science and pursues humanitarian ends. The businessperson wouldn't passionately invest time and energy in amassing wealth unless he or she was committed to success. The researcher wouldn't tirelessly experiment unless he or she trusted science. Regardless of the field or endeavor, everyone begins with an assumption. Assumptions are beliefs. And, believing is faith.

Without faith, no one would act on his or her beliefs. Faith compels believers and nonbelievers alike to pursue convictions. It is the substance behind remarkable discoveries, great accomplishments and miracles. Faith starts small and eventually explodes, erupting into life-long pursuits.

Faith is necessary for relationships too. Children naturally believe in the goodness of their parents. Employees trust employers to pay them at the end of the week.

In the broadest sense of the word: Faith is a belief in someone or something that compels a person to act in accordance with their belief. As faith increases, so does boldness. The disciples prayerfully waited for the promised Holy Spirit. **[Acts 1:12-14]** They hoped! When the Spirit filled the disciples, they experienced God first hand, and as never before. **[Acts 2:4]** Their faith was forever solidified. As a result, the disciples fearlessly testified. **[Acts 2:14-40, 4:13, 4:29]**

Within the kingdom of God, however, as faith increases action decreases. The power of faith takes over and performs its good work. **[Luke 17:6]** Striving entails flesh. Jesus, who was the pinnacle of faith, merely spoke and the elements obeyed Him. **[Mark 4:39]** Rest assured, however, regardless of the context or medium, abundant words indicate faithlessness, and even more disconcerting, lying. **[Proverbs 10:19]**

What or whom one places their faith in becomes paramount since interest determines actions. For example, if a person ultimately believes in himself, he acts according to self-interest. If a person ultimately believes in God, he acts in agreement with the Lord.

Jesus went to heal a dying girl. **[Luke 8:41]** Crowds followed and pushed against Him. **[Luke 8:45]** A woman in the crowd suffered from bleeding for twelve years because no one could heal her. **[Luke 8:43]** Possessing great faith, she pressed through the crowd, touched the edge of Jesus' cloak and received miraculous healing. **[Luke 8:44]**

The woman never lost hope, even after twelve years of disappointment. She refused to give up. She sought Jesus instead of another physician. The woman's tremendous faith compelled her to bold action and she pushed through the throng of people. And because of her tremendous faith, she required a mere touch in order to experience wholeness.

LOVE

Unconditional love is the most powerful force in the universe. Hope and faith find expression through love. Without divine love, nothing would exist. Love considers no sacrifice too great. True charity knows no boundaries. It forgets wrongs. People do not define love, but rather, love defines people. Folks carry the heavenly substance in their hearts: whether farmer, mother, child, cowboy, laborer, prophet, patriot, welder, athlete, writer, musician, mathematician, or teacher. Love transforms work into vocation, and even art. Prison bars bend before this eternal force. Fiery passion compels losers unto greatness. Even death acquiesces to love. **[Matthew 28:1-10]**

Jesus underscored two points throughout His ministry:

Love the Lord your God with all your heart and with all your soul, and with all your mind. This is the first and greatest commandment. And the second is like it: Love your neighbor as yourself. **[Matthew 22:37-38]**

If one wholeheartedly pursues these two commandments, everything else takes care of itself.

1 Corinthians 13, or The Love Chapter as it is commonly known, is arguably the most quoted passage in the Bible. Under the guidance of the Holy Spirit, Paul amplified the Lord's teaching and timelessly described love. There is absolutely no way to best scripture. Nevertheless, even after reading chapter 13, believers regularly overlook the heart of love.

Paul said, in verses **4** through **6**, what love is and isn't. He finalized his point in verse **7**: *"It always protects, always trusts, always hopes, always perseveres."* Notice the use of the term 'always.' The point being: Love is a steadfast, unwavering commitment. Even when opposed by impossibility, true love never capitulates.

Unconditional love equates to eternal commitment. Devotion represents maturity. Quitting or falling out of love is simply immature infatuation. Abiding love births intimacy. Intimacy is spiritual or heartfelt knowing. The lover intimately knows the beloved through ongoing, enduring relationship. Love burns bright and knows no end.

Throughout time, cultures the world over have propagated the myth of genius. Popular thought maintains a handful of extremely talented people are responsible for humankind's greatest discoveries and achievements. Geoff Colvin toppled that myth in his book, *Talent Is Overrated: What Really Separates World Class Performers from Everybody Else.* An incredible work ethic distinguishes history makers from others, and not innate talent or off-the-chart IQs. **[Colvin]** Relentless commitment can, and often does realize record-setting achievements. Passion translates into tenacious effort, and tenacious effort equates to commitment. Passionate love transcends mediocrity. The faithful go above and beyond, regardless of field, pursuit or relationship.

When a person loves, he commits himself to someone or something. Real commitment involves purposeful time, energy and effort. Runners clock miles. Musicians compose songs. Painters create art. Fathers nurture children. Husbands serve wives. Christians commune with the Father.

Half-heartedness stalls intimacy with God and others. The Lord is first and foremost Love, and He searches for committed lovers. Unreserved commitment is the only requirement for an ever maturing, inexhaustible relationship with God.

This revelation is imperative for all believers. Without commitment, and consequently intimacy, one's knowledge of God is relegated to hearsay, or at worst, ignorant chatter. Armchair quarterbacks are found everywhere, but especially in Institutional Christianity. If people rely on flawed ministers or naïve Christians for understanding, then they'll eventually fall away. In other words, one knows about God, rather than personally experiencing Him. Knowing about God collapses into a cold, sterile relationship of 'don'ts.' God becomes a distant, unconcerned First Cause or Deity. Only through intimate fellowship does one come to know God as He really is-- unfathomable Love.

Jesus was and is Love incarnate. He totally gave Himself to twelve friends for three years. In the end, one sold out and all deserted Him. **[Matthew 26:47-56]** Neither cowardice nor death could quench the Lord's commitment to His beloved disciples, or ultimately, humanity. Jesus fulfilled His own words, *"Greater love has no one than this, that he lay down his life for his friends."* **[John 15:13]** Except for Judas who hung himself, all were reinstated and commissioned. **[Matthew 27:5, 28:16-20]** Love never fails. **[1 Corinthians 13:8]**

In summary, personal experience is required for knowledge. Experience either enhances or taints awareness. An unshakeable belief, or hope, inspires folks onward. The hopeful believe there's got to be something more and continue to look beyond present circumstances. Likewise, faith acts in accordance with convictions. As fidelity increases so does boldness. Conversely, within the kingdom of God, great faith entails diminishing action. Hope and faith are dimensions of love. Love is unwavering commitment. Mature love, and therefore lasting relationship, creates intimacy, and with intimacy flow the deeper realms of knowledge.

MEANING

Humans generate meaning. Meaning is assigned value. Individuals assign value to anything and everything: a rock, the color red, coffee, a boyfriend, springtime, outhouses, a Snickers bar, sex, Cairo, the neighbor's cat, the Pacific, Picasso, guns, rain, flies, silver, cucumbers, cancer, and on and on. Values are endless too: good, bad, poor, great, unbelievable, so-so, take-it-or-leave-it, a six out of ten, can't stand it, can't live without it, a solid C, a tinker's dam, a waste of time, fa-getta-bout-it, unreal, etc. etc. And yet, how is meaning derived?

My wife and I recently spoke with a young man who believed people always lie. I found his perspective fascinating, and went on to reflect. I've lied on more than one occasion and I'm sure everyone else has too: whether as a child, an adult, or somewhere along the way. But, to maintain that folks are always lying is pure nonsense. Life would come to a screeching halt because no one could trust anyone else. My wife and I don't lie, nor do most people we know. So, according to this man's perspective, why does everyone lie?

I also know a boring middle-aged man. If I sit down with him for a cup of coffee, he talks for hours on end about himself. All I hear is 'blah-blah-blah' after fifteen minutes. I've confronted his bad manners, and yet, he continues lecturing others and me on his favorite subject.

Both examples indicate underlying values, or meaning. The young man believes everybody lies because he does. He must think, in some strange perverted way, lying benefits him. In turn, the boring middle-aged man focuses on himself. Individuals discuss what is important to them.

One's inner condition determines meaning. People are inherently self-centered. Consequently, meaning develops from personal interest. People naturally desire ease, but avoid difficulties.

But, when love enters it transforms. Charity counters, and proves antidotal to self-centeredness. Remember, love is an unwavering commitment to someone or something. True love, then, is other-centered rather than self-centered. A radical revaluing ensues. People and things take on an entirely new meaning: instead of hoarding money, it's given away; in-laws become parents; rejection turns into blessing; enemies are potential friends; books contain rich information; and past failure means future success.

As intimacy matures, knowledge grows. Only through an ongoing relationship, in good times and bad, can one truly appreciate another. Commitment reveals ever increasing dimensions of another's being, as well as one's self. Meaning evolves, and the ordinary becomes the extraordinary.

Paul said:

When I was a child, I talked like a child, I thought like a child, I reasoned like a child. When I became a man, I put childish ways behind me. Now we see in but a poor reflection as in a mirror; then we shall see face to face. Now I know in part; then I shall know fully, even as I am fully known. **[1 Corinthians 13:11-12]**

Children get offended and quit relationships. Children are fickle. Generally, the attitude is, 'What do I get out of it?' or 'What benefits me?' Children often evaluate relationships in terms of schoolyard status, rather than considering the needs of others. Immaturity destroys relationships. Sadly, there are multitudes of childish adults, believers and nonbelievers alike.

However, as children mature and grow in love, they take responsibility for themselves and others. This is adulthood-- caring for those entrusted to us. For the mature, difficulties only strengthen one's resolve and relationships. As Paul alluded to, though, believers never entirely arrive in this life, but grow throughout eternity.

Love must be viewed as a spectrum, rather than either/or. Hopefully, an infant's capacity for love differs from a teenager's, and a teenager's from a parent's. Even bad people love. **[Matthew 7:11]** Grade school addition is less complicated than high school trigonometry, and trigonometry is more straightforward than mind-bending physics. Only through unwavering commitment does one discover the greatness of others, or the beautiful symmetry of numbers. Only love knows.

Unbelievers and ignorant Christians impose either/or attitudes on others. Supposedly, when someone makes a   commitment to God, or anything else, he or she suddenly becomes a flawless expert. Reasonable people don't make those demands upon children, or adults for that matter. Yet, this is the very thing believers do to themselves and others. Maturity requires time. Patience and grace must be extended to all.

Love produces spiritual X-ray vision. The capacity for love heightens perception and unfolds layers of meaning. As superficiality recedes, essence comes into view. Essence is true meaning. Although no one is capable of perceiving in totality, nevertheless lovers can and do peer into essence.

Jesus, in reference to Himself, made this statement, *"Stop judging by mere appearances, and make a right judgment."* **[John 7:24]** The Lord's remarkable commonness caused the religious leaders to overlook His real identity. **[John 7:28-29]** From their perspective, greatness rode white horses and wore crowns. Because of Jesus' divine origins, He appeared dark and mysterious to the earthly minded. **[John 1:10]** Loveless hearts are incapable of genuine insight as evidenced by the Pharisees. **[John 5:41-44]**

Potent words are considered the force behind prophecy, and to a certain extent, correctly so. Life and death are in the power of the tongue. **[Proverbs 18:21]** However, prophetic words reveal a deeper truth. Love empowers lovers to see into the lives of others, and in turn, express God's heart. **[1 Corinthians 14:25]** Prophets were originally called seers, and for good reason; they saw into life's mysteries.

I've spoken kind, uplifting words to prostitutes, thugs, and blatant sinners on a number of occasions. Almost without exception, onlookers sigh or gasp. I know what they're thinking; 'He really missed it.' The fact of the matter is I've missed the mark many times. Nobody, and I mean absolutely nobody, is infallible. Nevertheless, folks confine their understanding to temporal circumstances and don't perceive goodness in others. God never intended anyone to be a prostitute or thug. Superficial assessments fail to recognize another's high calling, or essence. Everyone possesses divine purpose. Love doesn't see a whore, but a noble woman of God. Love doesn't see a gangster, but an evangelist. Love doesn't see a junkie, but a devoted father. Love serves to reveal the essence of others.

Scripture bores countless Christians. Many folks resort to liturgical readings or daily devotionals in order to stay faithful. Others haphazardly grind out a chapter here and there through shear will. A few memorize and recite pet verses. And for many individuals, the Bible doesn't even make sense.

Love empowers sight, but also creates openness. Openness is humility. Love communicates, and flows back and forth between lovers. Wherever love resides, so too does humility. Openness is the flip side of charity. Charity gives, but openness receives. The heavenly duo cannot be separated. Humility is slow to speak and quick to listen. If love is the husband, then humility is the wife. One completes the other. If loves sees, then humility hears.

Conversely, rigidity is pride. Pride fears and refuses to listen. Wherever pride exists, so does inflexibility. Know-it-alls, whether secular or religious, are nothing more than ignorant, insecure people. Rigidity retards knowledge. Fear deadbolts hearts. Inflexibility silences meaningful communication.

Hebrews 4:12 says,

For the word of God is living and active. Sharper than any double edged sword, it penetrates even to dividing soul and spirit, joints and marrow; it judges the thoughts and attitudes of the heart.

For years, I focused on what scripture did, rather than on what scripture is, or being. Scripture performed true to its claim by refuting naysayers and exposing hidden agendas. More importantly, however, scripture is living and active. In other words, scripture is a real living entity, and not merely a holy text, or a static document. The Bible is alive! Therefore, like any living, breathing entity, scripture communicates. The psalmist passionately loved scripture and proclaimed, *"The unfolding of your words gives light; it gives understanding to the simple."* **[Psalm 119:130]**

A dynamic, spiritual dance occurs between scripture and reader. The Bible responds to openness or humility. As one grows in humility, scripture unfolds itself and imparts greater revelation. Scripture and reader commit themselves to one another. Dry, dusty words are transformed into spiritual sustenance for the tender hearted. And, like any great lover, scripture increasingly yields itself before the beloved. The Bible's greatest treasures are yet to be mined.

And so, meaning is assigned value. People assign value to anything and everything. One's inner condition determines meaning. Since individuals are predisposed to self-centeredness, love proves antidotal and transforms meaning. Unwavering commitment, or love, peels back layers of superficiality and eventually reveals the essence of another. Love is not an either/or proposition, but a spectrum. Everyone possesses a high calling. Love and humility are bound together. Scripture is alive and responds to humility.

INTERPRETATION

Individuals are incapable of not interpreting. People draw conclusions from whomever and whatever they encounter. Interpretation is not a good thing or a bad thing in and of itself, but rather, it is an innate human function. Nevertheless, correct interpretation becomes extremely important when making critical, or life altering decisions. Misinterpretation leads to erroneous conclusions, which in turn proves detrimental to one's wellbeing.

Interpretation is the process of evaluating information. Meaning undergirds interpretation by assigning value to that being considered. And, as stated earlier, love, or a lack thereof, determines meaning.

In this day and age, God is pouring out His Spirit. **[Joel 2:28]** People from all walks of life are experiencing dreams and visions. It is truly amazing! Interestingly though, most dreams and visions are highly symbolic. God speaks through biblical idioms and pictures. These modes of communication are universal and transcend age, gender and ethnicity. Recipients are regularly required to search matters out.

God-inspired visions and dreams reveal specific circumstances and spiritual realities. Oftentimes, the truth convicts and proves difficult to accept, or even acknowledge. People pursue praise and disregard loving correction from others. Only the very mature readily embrace the Lord's discipline.

Since most believers don't dwell in unconditional Love, they purposely twist visions and dreams to favor themselves. The catchphrase is, 'God told me.' It's a hyper-spiritual way of expressing, 'Don't challenge me.' The fearful perceive God's unsettling revelations as negative, or even incriminating. Nothing could be further from the truth. God mercifully, but nevertheless disturbingly, divulges spiritual revelation through dreams and visions in order to prevent harm, provide direction, or alleviate potentially destructive attitudes and behaviors. Unless a person is spiritually in the know, he or she falls prey to demonic traps. The Father warns people. Knowledge is power.

The fearful interpret according to right or wrong. These individuals value rightness above and beyond truth. Pride pursues popularity and sidesteps integrity. Insecure people are self-serving and neglect neighbors. Often, the truth brings and necessitates change.

The beloved is secure in love, and therefore, he or she interprets according to truth. Truth supersedes personal accolades. Humility chooses integrity, and when the circumstances arise, fully acknowledges wrongdoing.

Consequently, interpretation is an innate human function and the process of evaluating information. Meaning undergirds the process by assigning value to that being considered. Love determines meaning.

Presently, God is pouring out His Spirit through dreams and visions. These modes of revelation are highly symbolic, and rooted in biblical idioms. The beloved interprets according to truth, while the fearful side with rightness. Humility chooses integrity above personal recognition.

UNDERSTANDING

One concise definition of understanding is: to stand under. I like that. The definition implies examination, and even humility. For anyone to possess a thorough knowledge of something, he or she must become a faithful student. And yet, just because a person commits himself to learning a subject matter does not necessarily entail understanding. There are first-rate contractors and bad carpenters. There are excellent chefs and poor cooks. There are great educators and substandard teachers. There are studio musicians and bar bands. Understanding involves much more than extensive learning.

Here again, love is critical. An unwavering commitment weathers the bad with the good. A person pursuing mastery is passionate, and even thrives during dry seasons. The lover does what he does because of who he is. Neither fame nor riches motivates, but rather, an unyielding love. Failure can and does contribute more to understanding than success. Insights are gleaned from anything and everywhere. A person of understanding is forever mindful of his or her passion. The beloved resides in the heart of the lover.

Mastery, in any field, perceives intent. Purpose inspires everything from dinner menus to fashion. Intent provides direction. A master chef grasps his restaurateur's dreams. A competent architect incorporates her client's style and values. A prophet knows the heart of the Father. Ease and flow occurs by understanding the overall scheme of things. The main thing stays the main thing.

Skill often becomes secondary. A young soldier may be able to out-shoot her superior, but she lacks the senior's battle savvy. A framer may be able to pound nails faster than his general contractor, but lacks the latter's extensive experience.

Understanding also involves proper relationship. Greater symmetry equates to greater order. Order is the stamp of humanity. Divine order is the stamp of God. The seasoned student understands intent, and in turn, he or she has acquired an awareness of what contributes to, and what detracts from the realization of a project.

Understanding is the ability to perceive purpose and proper relationships. An understanding person streamlines, and cuts frills. Understanding creates simplicity. Wherever disorder exists, understanding is noticeably absent. More is less. Complication is a sign of confusion. Understanding recognizes patterns, alleviates excess and channels value into purpose.

Therefore, one definition of understanding is: to stand under. However, extensive learning does not necessarily entail understanding. Love is critical to understanding. Passion pursues mastery. Dry seasons and failure are vital to understanding. The lover does what he does because of who he is. Mastery sees intent. Ease and flow occur by understanding the overall scheme of things. Skill often becomes secondary. Comprehension grasps proper relationship, or symmetry; in essence, what fits and what doesn't. Understanding is the ability to perceive purpose and proper relationship. It creates simplicity. More is less. Understanding recognizes patterns, alleviates excess and channels value into purpose.

SUMMARY

Thought was described throughout this chapter. People possess knowledge. They assign meaning to things. People are always interpreting and some even gain understanding. However, unless each mode of thought is transformed by love, all become skewed, and at best, severely limited. Skewed thinking translates into ungodly mindsets. When mental processes are devoid of love, deception occurs. Scripture is humanity's plumb line.

God is Love, and love determines healthy thought from the unhealthy. Folks need to know Him. We've seemingly returned to our starting point: *"The fear of the Lord is the beginning of wisdom, and knowledge of the Holy One is understanding."* **[Proverbs 9:10]** People develop ungodly mind-sets because they don't know Jesus. Most so-called Christians fail to understand God's ways. Again, understanding is the ability to perceive purpose and proper relationships.   Misunderstanding creates erroneous doctrines and causefusion.

The next chapter reveals who God really is.

Who God Really Is

"In many areas of understanding, none so much as in our under-standing of God, we bump up against a simplicity so profound that we must assign complexities to it to comprehend it at all. It is mindful of how we paste decals to a sliding glass door to keep from bumping our nose against it."

ROBERT BRAULT

Over the last couple of weeks I've been in constant dialogue with a dear friend. **[Ferraro]** Our discussions center on who God really is. We are convinced a distorted view of God has contributed to the demise of countless believers and nonbelievers alike. My friend and I cherish scripture, and therefore, we keep digging and looking for biblical precedence. The journey is thrilling. As of yet, I haven't undergone a paradigm shift. However, I've located missing pieces to the puzzle, and the picture is the clearest it's ever been.

I begin the chapter by discussing Jesus' relationship with the heavenly Father. Next, Old Testament causefusion is exposed and dismantled. A kingdom narrative follows. Lastly, I respond to poten-tial concerns and counterarguments.

JESUS AND THE FATHER

Jesus claimed that if someone saw Him, then, he or she saw the Father. **[John 14:9]** Jesus also said He and the Father were One. **[John 10:30, John 1:1]** This is the pinnacle of revelation. The Lord was the flesh and bones representation of the Father. Jesus' earthly ministry dispelled the mystery of who God really is! He tore the veil, and the ageless Mystery came into full view.

Jesus never turned anyone away. **[Mark 7:24-30]** Jesus extended mercy. **[Matthew 8:28-34]** Jesus refused to condemn. **[John 8:1-11]** Jesus embraced sinners. **[Matthew 9:9-13, Luke 7:36-50]** Jesus despised earthly riches. **[Luke 12:13-21]** Jesus loved the least of the least. **[Luke 23:32-43]** Jesus always forgave. **[Luke 23:34]** Jesus placed needs above rules. **[Matthew 12:1-14]** Jesus was kind and gentle. **[Mark 10:13-16]** Jesus rebuked the mean-spirited. **[Matthew 23]**

Now, consider your view of the heavenly Father. Did I just describe Him to you? Reflect and be honest with yourself. The overwhelming majority Christians would not describe God the same way I just described Jesus. Why is that? And yet, Jesus and the Father are One.

OLD TESTAMENT CAUSEFUSION

There is a single overarching lie that consistently distorts our perception of the Father. The causefusion stems from our erroneous understanding of the Old Testament. Unless one reads the Old Testament through the lens of the Lord Jesus Christ, he or she invariably comes to the conclusion God is a bloodthirsty killer who destroys anyone, including nations, that offend Him. Get on God's bad side, or break His law, and beware.

The sterile, but classic explanation is as follows: God is a righteous God, and therefore, He can't tolerate sin. People must pay for their sins, and in the OT, prior to the death and resurrection of Jesus, animal sacrifices substituted for the sinner's own blood. With the coming of Christ, a new dispensation began.

However, the bind remains. Christians are still left with a neurotic deity. Supposedly, God's righteous anger burned so hot towards sinful humanity that unless Jesus intervened everyone was doomed. Conversely, Jesus promenades through the countryside partying and freely forgiving adulteresses and thieves. Reconcile that? Was God playing bad cop/good cop? At this point, the pious toss bones: God is righteous, but loving; stern, but kind; holy, but forgiving. Cute, superficial responses fail to grasp the real discrepancy. There remains an impassable gulf dividing the God of the OT and the Savior of the NT. Or, is there?

Jesus went on to say, *"My Father is always at his work to this very day, and I, too, am working."* **[John 5:17]** God worked for a very long time. However, what was His work? Evidently, Jesus co-labored. God placed such significance upon His work that He sent Jesus to finish it. **[John 4:34]** Jesus also said, *"I tell you the truth, the Son can do nothing by himself; he can do only what he sees his Father doing, because whatever the Father does the Son also does."* **[John 5:19]**

Jesus bridged the impassable gulf with those statements. The life and words of Jesus are a perfect depiction of the heavenly Father. Remember how I described Jesus? Well, that's exactly who the Father is! Furthermore, God didn't change His mind, or take a self-imposed timeout upon Jesus' arrival. Rather, His work continued and culminated with His Son. When Jesus said, *"It is finished,"* the

Father's work ended. **[John 19:30]** God's attitude, values and ways have remained the same throughout eternity.

Consider the following: Have you ever worked a puzzle? Most have. Large, elaborate puzzles are extremely difficult to piece together until one sees the final picture. This is why the end product is plastered across the front of the box. After seeing the finished picture and keeping that image in mind, regardless of the difficulty, one can methodically reconstruct the puzzle. This principle parallels the discussion. By knowing that Jesus is the exact image of the Father, one can reread the OT from a completely different perspective. If a passage does not easily fit into a Christ-centered theology, oh well. Continue constructing your theology. One can modify and make adjustments if necessary, and eventually, troublesome and obstinate passages neatly fall into place. The Bible is the most beautiful book ever written. It's divine.

A KINGDOM NARRATIVE

In the beginning, God communed with humankind face to Face. **[Genesis 3:8]** He blessed Adam and Eve and gave them dominion over all things. **[Genesis 1:28-30]** Pure, undefiled love existed. There were no laws, except one; don't eat from the tree of knowledge of good and evil. **[Genesis 2:15-17]** Adam and Eve cared for God's sinless creation. This was God's kingdom, and it was good. **[Genesis 1:31]**

At the Fall, sin entered humanity and creation. **[Genesis 3, Romans 5:12-13]** Sin is self-centeredness. The Lord held Adam and Eve accountable, because, like all of us, they willfully transgressed.

[Genesis 3:16-19] Satan is the diabolical force and influence behind sin. **[1 John 3:7-8]** Sin is alive, and cruelly viral. **[Hufford 12/09/09]** Here are a few of its characteristics:

But if you do not do what is right, sin is crouching at your door; it desires to have you, but you must master it. **[Genesis 4:7]**

I tell you the truth, everyone who sins is a slave to sin. **[John 8:34]**

For sin shall not be your master, because you are not under law, but under grace. **[Romans 6:14]**

For the wages of sin is death, but the gift of God is eternal life in Christ Jesus our Lord. **[Romans 6:23]**

Then, after desire has conceived, it gives birth to sin; and sin, when it is full-grown, gives birth to death. **[James 1:15]**

Sin crouches, desires, rules, pays wages, births, and kills. Obviously, then, sin is not mindless, cosmic poison.

Satan evokes sin through lies and fear. **[John 8:44]** His kingdom was legally established at the Fall. At that point in time, Satan's dominion began over humankind and creation. Sin yields evil fruit: sexual immorality, impurity and debauchery; idolatry and witchcraft; hatred, discord, jealousy, fits of rage, selfish ambition, dissentions, factions and envy; drunkenness, orgies, and the like. **[Galatians 5:19-21]** Ultimately, sin produces death. **[Romans 6:23]** Satan exerts his will wherever death and destruction are found. **[John 10:10]**

Conversely, God is Love. **[1 John 4:16]** Love is the ultimate power in the kingdom of God, and for that matter, all of creation. It is committed, passionate, other-centered intentionality. Paul said:

Love is patient, love is kind. It does not envy, it does not boast, it is not proud. It is not rude, it is not self-seeking, it is not easily angered, it keeps no record of wrongs. Love does not delight in evil but rejoices with the truth. It always protects, always trusts, always hopes, always perseveres. Love never fails. **[1 Corinthians 13:4-8]**

Love is patient, kind, respectful, humble, other-focused, forgiving, truthful, protective, trustworthy, hopeful, persistent, and victorious. Love is the heart of God.

Jesus, the exact representation of the Father, embodied Love. His shed blood, or liquid love, trumps and covers all sin when appropriated by believers. The Father sent the promised Holy Spirit upon Christ's ascension. **[Acts 2:1-4]** The Holy Spirit lives in God's children. **[Romans 8:9]** God's indwelling presence, and therefore Love, produces godly fruit: love, joy, peace, patience, kindness, goodness, faithfulness, gentleness, and self-control. The Spirit gives life. **[Galatians 6:8]** Jesus came in order that believers might have life, and have it to the full. **[John 10:10]**

God's presence maintains order, and where His kingdom is firmly established, life dominates death. **[John 1:4]** God breathed into Adam and he lived. **[Genesis 2:7]** Abraham fellowshipped with God throughout his life, and when he was very old, the patriarch fathered children. **[Genesis 21:1-5, 25:1-4]** Aaron's staff sprouted, budded, blossomed and produced almonds while in the presence of the Lord. **[Numbers 17:8]** Moses communed with God and still possessed strength and sight at the very end of his days. **[Deuteronomy 34:7]** The prophet Elisha was so full of God that his bones brought a dead man back to life. **[2 Kings 13:21]** After Peter was empowered by the

Holy Spirit, his shadow healed people. **[Acts 5:15-16]** Handker-chiefs and aprons that touched Paul were laid upon the sick and they too were healed. **[Acts 19:11-12]** God is Life. **[2 Corinthians 3:6]**

Paul said of Jesus:

He is the image of the invisible God, the firstborn of all creation. For by him all things were created: things in heaven and on earth, visible and invisible, whether thrones or powers or rulers or authorities; all things were created by him and for him. He is before all things, and in him all things hold together. **[Colossians 1:15-17]**

Notice the last phrase, *"in him all things hold together."* The presence of God prevents all of creation from flying apart, and sliding into utter chaos. Jesus is creation's spiritual glue. Even the vilest sinners are recipients of His grace and goodness. **[Matthew 5:45]** More God equates to more life. Where God reins supreme, His glory unfolds and life explodes exponentially. **[2 Corinthians 3:18]** The garden experience is here and now, and not futuristic pie-in-the-sky. **[Colossians 1:13]**

Why did Jesus repeatedly proclaim and teach on the kingdom of God? **[Matthew 13, Mark 10:13-31, Luke 13:18-21, John 3:3 & 5]** For millennia, humankind lived under Satan's rule. What humanity considered normal, or life as usual, was in reality an insidious form of terror and imprisonment. Even now, after thousands of years, natural continues to be unnatural for lost humanity and ignorant Christians.

The Jews were called and purposed by the Father to reestablish the kingdom of God through the person of the Lord Jesus Christ. **[Matthew 15:24]** Jesus and His kingdom completely contradicted the worldly system and its devilish values. When the Lord said, *"Friend, your sins are forgiven"* **[Luke 5:20]**, He declared freedom and victory on behalf of humanity and creation. Remember, Satan's kingdom runs on sin and culminates in death. Jesus' earthly ministry began to erode Satan's authority. The kingdom of God was forever established with the Lord's death and resurrection.

Before balking, consider another passage. Jesus was tempted three times in the desert. **[Matthew 4:1-11]** The last temptation reads:

Again, the devil took him to a very high mountain and showed him all the kingdoms of the world and their splendor. All this I will give you, he said, if you will bow down and worship me. Jesus said to him, Away from me, Satan! For it is written: Worship the Lord your God, and serve him only. **[Matthew 4:8-10]**

Satan's wager was legitimate, otherwise, how could Jesus be tempted? Moreover, did those kingdoms encompass religious empires, and perhaps, even to this day, continue to remain under the devil's scheming ways, or at the very least his influence? I think so. The kingdom of God was reestablished, but has yet to be fully consummated.

CONCERNS AND COUNTERARGUMENTS
Why would God, Who is omnipotent, omniscient, and omnipresent, scuffle with a finite, exiled being like Satan?

First of all, unlike Star Wars, there is no dualistic, cosmic war between good and evil; God wins and light dispels darkness, always. However, love, beyond human comprehension, consumed the Father. God paid the ultimate price, His Son's life, in order to free humanity from satanic tyranny. God was lovesick and couldn't live without His beloved.

Secondly, God does not lie, cheat or murder when opposed by liars, cheaters and murderers. The Father loves, is fair, just, honest and truthful, regardless of persons, entities and circumstances. Jesus said, *"No one is good--except God alone."* **[Mark 10:18]** And James said, *"When tempted, no one should say, "God is tempting me." For God cannot be tempted by evil, nor does he tempt anyone..."* **[James 1:13]** Amen.

What about all the killing in the OT?

Consider the Egyptians and the Canaanites whom the Israelites displaced. God had an unusual conversation with father Abraham in **Genesis 15:12-16**,

Then the Lord said to him, Know for certain that your descendants will be strangers in a country not their own, and they will be enslaved and mistreated four hundred years. But I will punish the nation they serve as slaves, and afterward they will come out with great possessions. You, however, will go to your fathers in peace and be buried at a good old age. In the fourth generation your descendants will come back here, for the sins of the Amorites has not reached its full measure.

The Egyptians enslaved and even murdered the Israelites for over four hundred years. **[Exodus 1]** God was unquestionably patient and long-suffering with the Egyptians, almost to the detriment of His children, the Israelites. Think of the situation this way: Rich and powerful neighbors grabbed your children and made them slaves. When angered or threatened, these same neighbors believed it was their right to kill your children if they so chose. On top of that, your great, great grandfather made your neighbors rich and powerful. **[Genesis 47:13-26]** Only a coward would stand by and watch. And yet, God was slow to anger, not only demonstrating His love and kindness for the Israelites, but also, for the Egyptians.

Scripture also says, *"…for the sins of the Amorites has not reached its full measure."* The Amorites were bent on sinning. Four hundred years is a long time. Moreover, in keeping with the character of God, He did not leave the Amorites without witness or prophetic voice. God warned Nineveh. **[Jonah]** Why wouldn't He warn the Amorites? Israel wasn't the only nation with prophets who knew God. **[Numbers 22-24]** The Lord takes no pleasure in the death of anyone, including the wicked. **[Ezekiel 33:11]** Lastly, there is a maturing to sin. When sin reaches later stages, or adulthood, death ensues. **[James 1:15]** The sins of the Amorites filled up.

How does one account for all those bloody sacrifices, or the law? God still appears narcissistic and bloodthirsty.

God clothed Adam and Eve in animal skins after they sinned. **[Genesis 3:21]** Did those animals represent the first sacrifice? Although scripture remains ambiguous, the conjecture is not without merit. God desires believers to search matters out and discover truth.

If a sacrifice was made, who offered it? Adam and Eve? Since God provided skins, probably not. God is the only alternative.

An all-important question arises: Who received the offering? God? Did God burn with such anger He required a shot of blood to calm Himself? Hardly. The Father's unconditional love never waned.

A much more plausible explanation emerges. God sacrificed animals on behalf of Adam and Eve to appease the blood lust of Satan. Remember, God is Life, but Satan deals death. After sinning, Adam and Eve came under the authority of Satan, and therefore, they were subject to his rules. Satan's new subjects, Adam and Eve and their offspring, paid tribute with life, or blood. Thus, long before Christ's incarnation, the heavenly Father interceded on behalf of lost humanity.

Later, Cain and Abel made offerings as well. Cain provided an unacceptable offering from the ground, while Abel's came from his flocks and proved acceptable. **[Genesis 4:1-5]** The Bible says their offerings were made to the Lord. **[Genesis 4:3-5]** Interestingly, scripture also says:

I have no need of a bull from your stall or of goats from your pens, for every animal of the forest is mine, and the cattle on a thousand hills. I know every bird in the mountains, and the creatures of the field are mine. If I were hungry I would not tell you, for the world is mine, and all that is in it. Do I eat the flesh of bulls, or drink the blood of goats? **[Psalm 50:9-13]**

You do not delight in sacrifice, or I would bring it; you do not take pleasure in burnt offerings. **[Psalm 51:16]**

The multitude of your sacrifices--what are they to me? says the Lord. I have more than enough of burnt offerings, of rams and the fat of fattened animals; I have no pleasure in the blood of bulls and lambs and goats. **[Isaiah 1:11]**

Is there a total contradiction? Or, maybe over time, God became sick of burnt fur and blood?

Darin Hufford makes a profound and fascinating point: There is a vast difference between bringing an offering 'to' God versus making an offering 'for' God. **[Hufford 12/09/09]** Although Cain and Abel brought offerings to God, their offerings were intended for sin. And, never forget, Satan is the dark force behind sin.

The Lord warned Cain,

If you do what is right, will you not be accepted? But if you do not do what is right, sin is crouching at your door; it desires to have you, but you must master it. **[Genesis 4:7]**

Notice the tone. God did not issue an 'or else' ultimatum. Rather, His warning demonstrated caution and even encouragement.

Throughout history, Satan attempted to annihilate God's people and His chosen One. **[Esther, Matthew 2:1-19]** In response, God codified the legal conditions of sin in the Mosaic Law. The law fleshed out the dangers sin imposed on God's people. The law was meaningless apart from sin. **[Romans 3:20]** God shielded His children from harm.

Jesus was the final sin offering. The Father didn't require the blood of His only begotten Son. How absurd! God is not a blood merchant like Molech. **[Leviticus 18:21]** Why would God forbid the Israelites, and later on gentile believers, from eating blood while He supposedly consumed it daily? **[Deuteronomy 12:23-24, Acts**

15:20, Leviticus 1:1-17] God would be the greatest hypocrite of all. But, He's not.

Jesus became sin for lost humanity. **[2 Corinthians 5:21]** The Lord accomplished what the law was powerless to do, namely, the destruction of the devil's works. **[1 John 3:8]** Not only did Jesus' sacrifice upend Satan's earthly kingdom, but it also satisfied legal requirements for all of creation, even extending to the temple of God in heaven. **[Hebrews 9:23-28]**

Every believer can and should live free from the power of sin. **[1 John 5:18]** Jesus is Lord, and therefore Satan's rule ended. The beloved's righteousness is found in Jesus alone. **[Romans 5:18-19]** The accusations of the prince of the world are empty and unfounded, and he lost audience with the Father. **[Revelation 12:10-12]** By embracing Jesus as Lord and Savior, believers are adopted into the holy family of God, and since they are joint heirs with Jesus, all rights and privileges of sonship belong to them as well. **[Galatians 4:1-7]** Believers are seated in the heavenlies with the Lord. **[Ephesians 2:6-7]** Communion with the Father was restored. **[1 John 1:3]**

God is judging the world since He can no longer tolerate humanity's extreme wickedness.

Prophetic dooms-dayers are blaming God, and often times smugly, with worldwide disasters. Supposedly, just like in the days of Sodom and Gomorrah, God is fed up. However, nothing could be further from the truth. This is classic causefusion.

What is God's judgment?

Jesus said,

Now is the time for judgment on this world; now the prince of this world will be driven out. But I, when I am lifted up from the earth, will draw all men to myself. **[John 12:31-32]**

According to this passage, then, God's judgment entails Jesus' crucifixion. The rulers of this world who crucified the pure, sinless Lamb of God stood condemned, and in turn, forfeited their reign over humanity and creation. **[1 Corinthians 2:8]** While the cross exposed Satan, and crushed his stolen power, it also demonstrated the love of God through Jesus' sacrifice. **[Colossians 2:15, 1 Corinthians]**

When the King of kings, or the Lord Jesus Christ, came into the world, He brought and established His kingdom. In so doing, God judged the world. The kingdom of God absolutely opposes all other kingdoms. Jesus conquered the world with love, life and truth. **[1 John 4:16, John 1:4, 17]** His blood covers all sin. **[Colossians 1:20]** Those who belong to the kingdom of God are sealed with the Spirit of Christ, and therefore, live according to heavenly realities. **[Ephesians 1:13]** At the end of the age, there will be a separation between those sealed with the Holy Spirit, and those who aren't. **[Matthew 13:40-43, 49-50]**

Reflect for a moment. Why would God destroy humanity, especially after His Son died for us? Are the sins of lost humanity greater than the blood of the Lord Jesus Christ? Is God a moody, unstable deity? One moment He's blissfully happy, and in the next, He's snorting mad, ready to murder. How can God command believers to forgive others, even enemies, and yet, according to dooms-dayers,

He's unwilling to do so? **[Luke 6:27-36]** Once again, God would epitomize hypocrisy.

Remember, death and destruction are the sole domain of Satan. He hates humanity and all of creation. The devil is committed to the total ruination of everyone and everything.

God pleads with His beloved, but does not demand. Love refuses to control or coerce. Freedom is paramount to love; individuals can have whatever they want. God does not violate hearts. Consequently, if one chooses to reject God's tender advances, he or she can.

As people, or even nations, reject God, they align themselves with darkness. Satan's kingdom is devoid of grace and mercy. God honors the desires of others, and withdraws or pulls back His presence. In turn, Satan steps forward, and true to his nature, kills. Satan destroys when given a foothold. **[Ephesians 4:25-28]** Life and order deteriorate without the presence of God.

SUMMARY

Jesus is the exact representation of God. He and the Father are One. A misreading of the Old Testament has created causefusion among believers and unbelievers alike. God is regularly viewed as angry and bloodthirsty. Only through the person of the Lord Jesus Christ can the Old Testament be properly understood. Jesus did what He saw the Father doing. God interceded on behalf of His beloved throughout time by sacrificing, instructing, instituting the law and sending His only begotten Son, the Lord Jesus Christ.

At the Fall, sin entered creation, and Satan established his kingdom. Sin is self-centeredness. Satan evokes sin. It is a living, diabolical force that crouches, desires, rules, pays wages, births, and ultimately brings about death. Satan exacted tribute from humanity by requiring life, or blood. For millennia, he terrorized, and what humanity considered normal was in actuality devilish imprisonment.

The Lord Jesus Christ, or God incarnate, lived, preached and reintroduced the kingdom of God. God judged the world by sending His Son, and in so doing, defeated all temporal, worldly powers. Jesus' death and resurrection was the final sin offering that crushed the works of the devil. His blood covers any and all sin. Wherever the kingdom of God is firmly established, life and order reign. There is no cosmic battle between good and evil; light always dispels darkness. What was once lost, intimacy with God, is now restored. A heavenly or Edenic life is available to all who call Jesus Lord and Savior.

God is Love. Love is committed, passionate, other-centered intentionality and the most powerful force in all of existence. Love is patient, kind, respectful, humble, other-focused, forgiving, truthful, protective, trustworthy, hopeful, persistent and victorious. The Holy Spirit is the seal of God. All those who know Jesus as Lord and Savior possess the Spirit of Christ.

The Spirit gives life.

A Second Look at Jezebel and the Antichrist Spirit

"It's not what you think it is."
WALTER JUSTICE

Over the years, I've heard countless warnings concerning the spirit of Jezebel. For angry fire-and-brimstone types, anyone who wears make-up or jewelry is a Jezebel. Others direct their allegations toward single, divorced women. Some think Jezebel only targets spiritual leadership. And still others, both men and women, don't even believe a Jezebel spirit exists, let alone an antichrist spirit.

The classic Jezebelian profile is as follows: A demonic spirit that seeks wounded, unsuspecting human hosts, primarily women but also men, and employs whatever evil means necessary to maintain control and power over others. The so-called experts, if there are such people, often use these words and phrases when describing the spirit and its host: proud, controlling, power-hungry, domineering, seductive, intimidating, manipulative, lying, immoral, flattery, pants-in-the-family, ruthless, positioning, subversive, undermining, vicious, man-hater, feminist, vengeful, blackmail, kiss-up, sensual, selfishness, lustful, compromise, behind-the-scenes, covert, gossip, character assassination, arrogant, demeaning, crass and brazen.

Generalizations are generalizations. Broad, loose definitions often fail to capture essence or fundamental nature. Most folks could stamp a number of the previous characterizations on someone they know, or perhaps, even on themselves. And yet, just because a person manipulates or gossips does not necessarily mean he or she is a Jezebel. No, the waters are murkier than previously realized.

This chapter begins by considering demonic realities. I then look at Jezebel throughout the ages. Next, **Revelation 2:18-29**, or the letter to the Church in Thyatira is discussed and tied directly to the antichrist spirit.

DEMONIC REALITIES

Evil spirits tormented people. **[Matthew 9:32-33]** Jesus freed captives wherever He went. If one peruses the Gospels, approximately one third of Jesus' ministry involved casting out demons. That's a lot. And yet, today, in the West, few believers have ever cast out a single demon. How is that? Do hymnals and pews repulse demons? Or, do these shadowy entities gravitate towards primitive cultures and archaic rituals because iPhones and computers are kryptonite for them? Jesus said:

And these signs will accompany those who believe: In my name they will drive out demons; they will speak in new tongues; they will pick up snakes with their hands; and when they drink deadly poison, it will not hurt them at all; they will place their hands on sick people, and they will get well. **[Mark 16:17-18]**

Was the Lord's declaration confined to first century believers, or did it also apply to the twenty-first century church? Perhaps believers get to pick and choose what they want to do and not do? The Lord's declaration transcended time, race and culture.

According to the western scientific mind, Jesus was a historical figure and a byproduct of His time. Superstitious people, then and now, ignorantly attribute sickness and disease to dark, unseen powers. Science has supposedly proven mental and bodily ailments are rooted in biological disparities. One visits the doctor if he or she becomes sick. Physicians are modernity's new high priests.

It is absolutely wrong-headed and unbiblical to infer all sickness originates from sin, or demonic affliction. **[John 9:1-3]** People make poor choices. Some injure themselves playing sports. Others are exposed to toxic substances. Accidents happen. The list is endless. And thankfully medical professionals rescue us.

However, there are strange ailments that seemingly defy explanation. Weird events occur. Though the cause remains a mystery, science and the medical community continues to name these elusive events and diseases; people feel better when they can grab hold of something. Patient frustration skyrockets if a pill or a shot doesn't alleviate discomfort or sickness. Surgeries are last resort. Western society is medically indoctrinated, myself included.

And yet, the Lord Jesus Christ, from Whom all things were created, and for Whom all things were made, chased away evil spirits. **[Colossians 1:16]** How can true believers do any different? Since Jesus is Lord, and true believers follow Him, the standard was and is the same-- whatever Jesus did, we do.

Jesus said:

How can Satan drive out Satan? If a kingdom is divided against itself, that kingdom cannot stand. If a house is divided against itself, that house cannot stand. And if Satan opposes himself and is divided, he cannot stand; his end has come. In fact, no one can enter a strong man's house and carry off his possessions unless he first ties up the strongman. Then he can rob his house. **[Mark 3:23-27]**

The Lord responded in the form of parables to demonic allegations leveled against him. **[Mark 3:22]** Jesus healed people and the religious establishment despised him. The Pharisees and Sadducees portrayed themselves as the real representatives of God, and nobody was to upstage them, especially not a hillbilly from Galilee.

The Old Testament greats never cast out demons. Remember the kingdom narrative? Since Satan and his demonic cohorts governed, the ancients were forced into spiritual slavery. Torment and death reigned. Animal sacrifices and blood appeased satanic tyranny and temporarily staved off death.

Demonic affliction was diverse and wide. An evil spirit ignited Saul's anger and he tried to kill David. **[1 Samuel 18:10-11]** A lying spirit spoke through prophets, deceived Ahab and caused a war. **[1 Kings 22:19-23]** Satan murdered Job's family, stole the patriarch's wealth and shattered his health. **[Job 1 & 2]** The devil accused Joshua. **[Zechariah 3:1]** The demoniac was driven to insanity, broke chains and forced to live in tombs. **[Luke 8:26-39]** An evil spirit crippled a woman. **[Luke 13:10-13]** After Satan entered Judas Iscariot, he betrayed Jesus. **[Luke 22:3-6]** A demon left a child mute, triggered convulsions and attempted to murder him. **[Mark 9:14-27]** Another spirit shrieked and violently shook a man. **[Mark 1:23-26]** A demon gave a slave girl the ability to fortune-tell and make money for her masters. **[Acts 16:16-18]** The seven sons of Sceva were brutally beaten by a demon-possessed man. **[Acts 19:13-16]**

Therefore, demons affect hosts by stirring their emotions, inciting anger, murdering, lying, deceiving, starting wars, stealing, destroying health, accusing, creating mental instability and insanity, causing squalor, depriving of natural faculties, betraying, convulsing, shrieking and endowing them with supernatural powers and strength.

Since demons belong to the kingdom of darkness, they gravitate towards sin. Garbage lures rats. Manure attracts flies. Sin entices demons. Sin is self-centeredness.

Jesus said:

For from within, out of men's hearts, come evil thoughts, sexual immorality, theft, murder, adultery, greed, malice, deceit, lewdness, envy, slander, arrogance and folly. **[Mark 6:21]**

Paul continued:

People will be lovers of themselves, lovers of money, boastful, proud, abusive, disobedient to their parents, ungrateful, unholy, without love, unforgiving, slanderous, without self-control, brutal, no lovers of the good, treacherous, rash, conceited, lovers of pleasure rather than lovers of God... **[2 Timothy 3:2-4]**

And the fruit thereof:

... sexual immorality, impurity and debauchery; idolatry and witchcraft; hatred, discord, jealousy, fits of rage, selfish ambition, dissensions, factions and envy; drunkenness, orgies, and the like. **[Galatians 5:19-21]**

Again, sin entices demons. Once a demon finds a host, or spiritual home, it takes up residence. **[Luke 11:24]** Demons intensify and amplify sin, and in so doing, further the kingdom of darkness. Some are worse than others, and they apparently run in packs or have like-minded associations. For example, anger and murder work together. **[Luke 11:26]** All are totally committed to the ruination of their host and everyone else.

Ongoing, heated debate continues between believers as to whether Christians can be demonized. Oppression or possession? Which is it? Proponents of demonization offer convincing personal testimonials. Opponents cite little or no scriptural support for Christian deliverance. A few factors must be taken into account. First of all, how one frames something is extremely important. Framing determines picture, and therefore, focus. Boundaries include or exclude subject matter.

Is oppression versus possession the right frame? No. Jesus depicted demons as strongmen. **[Luke 11:21-22]** Consequently, demons are spiritual bullies who exert their desires upon weak and unsuspecting victims, believers and unbelievers alike. The natural and spiritual parallel each other. **[1 Corinthians 15:44-45]** Schoolyard bullies steal milk money. Others throw rocks at houses and cars. Older bullies whoop on little kids. Thugs burglarize. Organized crews rape, terrorize and murder.

Demons act the same way, and they undoubtedly represent the motivation behind flesh and bone bullies. There are degrees of wickedness. Demons gobble up as much spiritual ground as possible. Wicked spirits join forces against good.

Where have all these foul spirits gone? Are they huddled together on an island in the South Pacific? The jungles of Africa? Maybe they're roaming through the Nevada desert?

The modern mind, and therefore advanced science, often addresses symptoms rather than root causes. Individuals learn to cope with struggles instead of overcoming. This is why a number of people must take certain medications for the rest of their lives. Others spend years in counseling. A few seem to be the unluckiest people in the world; when something can go wrong, it does. Many are closet addicts. Some are unnaturally accident-prone. So, what's really going on? Where's the victory? Could there be a spiritual bully lurking in the background? Perhaps.

Here's another important factor. Today, when a person becomes a Christian, she merely raises her hand and repeats a silent prayer. The newbie is registered in the church books and the pastor adds another notch to his spiritual gun. The new Christian shows up the following Sunday, and nothing has changed. In fact, nothing ever changes.

As was previously demonstrated, if a person is not a child of God, then he belongs to the kingdom of darkness. Sinful people attract demons. Not all demons murder or fortune-tell. Many intensify and amplify greed, lying, envy, sickness, jealousy, lust, hatred, rebellion, contempt, gossip, manipulation, fear, dissensions, factions, slander and immorality. Why aren't these issues discerned and addressed during one's salvation experience? Are so-called Christians even repenting? Interestingly, the Gospels indicate folks were baptized before they became believers. **[Matthew 3:1-6]** Are these so-called Christians even saved? Or, are they carrying spiritual baggage, including demons, from their previous lives? Perhaps, as alluded to a moment ago, nothing changes, and life goes on as before. Sadly, there appears to be no line of demarcation between believer and unbeliever.

Christians mystify spiritual realities too. Supposedly, only trained, seasoned professionals can discern evil spirits. Really? If one constantly burns with rage, and this person has confessed and renounced his struggles to fellow believers, maybe he's wrestling with a spirit of anger. **[Ephesians 6:12]** Perhaps someone else is a hypochondriac and terrified of dying. Is a spirit of fear tormenting her?

Fish swim. Birds fly. A demon of anger incites rage. A spirit of fear terrifies. Simple.

The Lord Jesus Christ, or the Son of God, overpowered the devil and all his demonic minions. **[Luke 11:20]** Those who profess Jesus as Lord and Savior are joint heirs with Him. **[Galatians 4:4-7]** The Spirit of Christ empowers true believers and they follow His example. **[1 John 2:6, Mark 16:17-18]** All believers are called to emulate the Lord's life, values and ministry--including casting out demons. **[Ephesians 5:1-2]** Failure to do so equates to outright disobedience and an unbiblical lifestyle. If Jesus cast out demons, then so too should His disciples.

Consequently, the Lord cast out demons wherever He went. Jesus said that whosoever believed would cast out demons too. **[Mark 16:17-18]** And yet, today, in the West, few believers exercise this ministry.

Science has supposedly proven mental and bodily ailments are rooted in biological disparities. Scripture doesn't teach that all sickness originates from sin, or demonic affliction. [John 9:1-3]

Nevertheless, many strange ailments and weird events defy scientific explanation.

The Old Testament greats never cast out demons because Jesus had yet to arrive and establish His kingdom. Demonic affliction is wide and diverse. These spirits affect emotions, incite anger, murder, lie, deceive, start wars, steal, destroy health, accuse, create mental instability and insanity, cause squalor, deprive natural faculties, betray, convulse, shriek and provide supernatural powers and strength. Demons gravitate towards sin. Sin is self-centeredness. Once a demon finds a spiritual home, it takes up residence. Demons run in packs.

Can Christians be demonized? The question is framed incorrectly. Jesus depicted demons as strongmen. **[Luke 11:21-22]** Demons are spiritual bullies and some are worse than others. People learn to cope with struggles instead of overcoming them. Multitudes of so-called Christians may not even be saved, and many, in all likelihood, continue carrying old spiritual baggage. Demonic personalities find expression through their hosts.

All believers are called to emulate Jesus' life, values and ministry-- including casting out demons. **[Ephesians 5:1-2]**

JEZEBEL THROUGHOUT THE AGES

A sinister personality keeps emerging throughout the ages. This personality runs kingdoms, kills prophets, seduces leaders, creates factions, preys upon the weak, promotes self, garners followings and craves unquestionable power. The unsuspecting and naive often dismiss Jezebel and relegate this evil spirit to human depravity. The naive explain her away by saying, 'Absolute power corrupts absolutely.' However, absolute power requires supernatural empowerment. Sin attracts demons, and extreme sin entices rulers in high places. Wherever people are controlled and dominated, whether in marriage, church, business, or government, rest assured, Jezebel is working. It rebels against and usurps God's ordained order and authority. Women want to be men, and men act like women. Leaders demand allegiance and obedience. Ministers use people. Businesses enslave. Husbands abuse wives. Wives control husbands. Jezebel's wickedness is systemic, and affects every segment of society.

God chose Moses to lead the Israelites. **[Exodus 3:10]** Miriam undermined her brother's authority. **[Numbers 12:2]** Korah led a full-blown rebellion against Moses. **[Numbers 16:1-3]** Delilah used her sexual prowess to subdue Samson. **[Judges 16:1-22]** Absalom stole the hearts of the Israelites from his father, David. **[2 Samuel 15:6]**

This dark, time-migrating spirit of control found supremacy and full expression in the person of Jezebel. **[1 Kings 16:31]** Because Jezebel fully gave herself to this evil entity, the two became intimately intertwined and their individual personas could no longer be distinguished. The demonic ruler sought pure, unbridled selfish ambition, and discovered that trait in Jezebel. She was the ideal host and wholeheartedly embodied an insatiable desire for preeminence; hence, the evil spirit's name.

King Ahab married Jezebel and began worshipping foreign gods. **[1 Kings 16:31-33]** He may have been king, but the queen was the real power. Ahab abdicated his roles of headship, husband and king to Jezebel. **[Ephesians 5:23, 1 Chronicles 11:2]** She wanted the throne and Ahab complied with her wishes. God ordained order and authority capsized.

It is inversion and perversion and wrong. Naysayers smirk and say something like, 'She's the neck that turns the head.' or 'She wears the pants-in-the-family.' The spiritually ignorant consistently portray Jezebels as young hotties bedding down unsuspecting old fools, and later on, blackmailing them. Yes, this behavior typifies Jezebel too. However, immorality and threats are mere stepping-stones. The evil spirit and its human partner thirst for power. Mature Jezebels call shots. A Jezebel's ultimate goal is to lord over others.

I remember ministering to a couple years ago. They were classic Ahab/Jezebel. The wife, as a young woman, stuffed socks down her pants pretending to have a 'package.' Her facial features and de-meanor were unusually masculine, and from a distance, people mistook her for a man. Her husband was big, tall and strong. Even so, when this guy turned his head, and made certain expressions, he strongly resembled a woman. I later learned that he enjoyed dressing up in women's clothing.

During ministry, the spiritual battle for the wife's soul seemingly came to a standstill. Her voice changed back and forth between normal and a guttural growl. I felt the Lord prompt me to put my face on her feet and pray. The moment I did, she supernaturally levitated from her seat and screamed. She described claws digging into her back. Jezebel hates humility. The woman and her husband were eventually freed and hopefully remain free.

A person's role and function shapes his or her values, look, speech and mannerisms. Good kids morph into gangsters while living the life. Housewives immerse themselves in family and become motherly. Executives do business and exude professionalism. Musicians champion self-expression and appear different.

I lived off a motorcycle for several years. When I put on my leathers, and climbed on my Harley, I was transformed into a modern day cowboy and all that accompanied that lifestyle. My role was biker and I became one.

A friend of mine spent virtually his entire life incarcerated. He's of Mexican descent: short, flat featured, covered in tattoos, brown eyes, and dark complected and black hair. I'm of northern European descent: tall, one tattoo, sharp   featured, blue eyes, fair, and bald. I've never been to prison. We're almost the exact opposites.

On one occasion, while visiting my friend, he pulled out his most recent prison card. He pointed to the picture and asked his four year old daughter, "Who's that?" She replied, "That's Mr. Justice." I was shocked. When I chose the role of biker, a spirit engulfed my being and changed me into an outlaw. An unpretentious little girl saw the truth.

According to some, Jezebel needs Ahab. Not really. The two compliment, but one (Ahab) does not necessitate the other (Jezebel). Whether a predator victimizes or not, he or she is still predatory. Whether a wolf feasts on venison or not, it continues hunting. Fire burns brighter with gasoline. Likewise, Jezebel thrives on passivity. She walks over human doormats in her quest for supremacy. Jezebel literally means "non-cohabitant." **[Jackson 53]**

The spirit of Jezebel resurfaced in the wicked queen's own daughter, Athaliah. She was queen without king, and like her mother, pursued unquestionable authority by almost murdering the entire royal family. **[2 Kings 11:1-3]** Herodias fell under Jezebel's spell too and killed John the Baptist. **[Matthew 14:3-12]**

And so, a sinister personality that desires unquestionable power keeps emerging throughout the ages. Sin attracts demons and extreme sin entices rulers in high places. The spirit of Jezebel is working wherever folks are controlled and dominated. It usurps God ordained order and authority.

This controlling, time migrating spirit used Miriam, Korah, Delilah and Absalom to rebel against God's chosen vessels. It found full expression and a perfect home in queen Jezebel who embodied an insatiable desire for preeminence. She represented the real force behind king Ahab's throne. Ahab/Jezebel relationships are inverted and perverted, and wrong.

A person's role and function shapes his or her values, look, speech and mannerisms. Jezebels often look and act like men. Conversely, Ahabs take on distinctly feminine roles. The two compliment, but Jezebels can and do exist independently of Ahabs.

The spirit of Jezebel resurfaced in the persons of Athaliah and Herodias.

REVELATION 2:18-29... THE CHURCH OF THYATIRA
Jesus said:

To the angel of the church in Thyatira write; These are the words of the Son of God, whose eyes are like blazing fire and whose feet are like burnished bronze. I know your deeds, your love and faith, your service and perseverance, and that you are now doing more than you did at first. Nevertheless, I have this against you: You tolerate that woman Jezebel who calls herself a prophetess. By her teaching she misleads my servants into sexual immorality and the eating of food sacrificed to idols. I have given her time to repent of her immorality, but she is unwilling. So I will cast her on a bed of suffering, and I will make those who commit adultery with her suffer intensely, unless they repent of her ways. I will strike her children dead. Then all the churches will know that I am he who searches hearts and minds, and I will repay each of you according to your deeds. Now I say to the rest of you in Thyatira, to you who do not hold to her teaching and have not learned Satan's so-called deep secrets (I will not impose any other burden on you): Only hold on to what you have until I come. To him who overcomes and does my will to the end, I will give authority over the nations--He will rule them with an iron scepter; he will dash them to pieces like pottery--just as I have received authority from my Father. I will also give him the morning star. He who has an ear, let him hear what the Spirit says to the churches. **[Revelation 2:18-29]**

The Lord presented Himself to the church of Thyatira as the Son of God, whose eyes are like blazing fire and whose feet are like burnished bronze. A person's image and demeanor signals his or her intention. If a person arrives at an accident scene in a police uniform, she's probably on official business. Conversely, if a person shows up at his neighbor's doorstep with a pizza and a twelve pack in hand, he might want to watch the college game on his friend's big screen.

Jesus portrayed Himself as the Son of God, and by doing so, He summoned heaven's authority. His Lordship issued warning. Likening His eyes to blazing fire substantiates this assertion. Spiritual sight penetrates hidden agendas. **[Psalm 139:1-3]** Fire purifies. **[Malachi 3:2-5]** The Lord looked far beyond the religious words and practices of the Thyatirans.

Feet like burnished bronze also lend support to this claim. Feet imply mobility and conduct. Most folks have heard the phrase, 'Walk the walk.' Bronze speaks of divine judgment in scripture. **[Deuteronomy 28:23]** The term burnished is another way of saying polished. The thought implies readiness and activity. For example, people polish good silverware in preparation for special occasions. When combined, the phrase *feet like burnished bronze* alludes to active judgment. Jesus evaluated the Thyatiran's faith. However, unlike the spiritually immature, Jesus did not assess according to mere appearances. He saw the Thyatiran's motives and divinely appraised their deeds.

The spiritually immature portray others as completely bad or good. Polarization is wrong-spirited. Ignorance resorts to black and white. The fearful are rigid, refuse to listen or discern nuances. Fear, and its evil mate pride, is the diabolical force behind racism. And so, everyone who belongs to a certain people group, regardless of talents, gifts, or contributions, is automatically deemed inferior. Pride and fear undergird political correctness as well. The politically correct fear others and consequently the label of intolerance, or the perception of being less than enlightened. But, as Jesus demonstrated, there is a time and place for speaking the truth in love. **[Matthew 23:5-36]**

Institutional Christianity mirrors the church of Thyatira. Jesus saw the good and stated, *"I know your deeds, your love and faith, your service and perseverance, and that you are now doing more than you did at first."* The Lord's exhortation was timeless. Today, true believers are pressing onward and upward. Many live sacrificial lives. As I tell family and friends, "There are good people wherever you go."

Even so, darkness crept into the ancient church. Jesus charged, *"Nevertheless, I have this against you: You tolerate that woman Jezebel, who calls herself a prophetess. By her teaching she misleads my servants into sexual immorality and the eating of food sacrificed to idols."*

Notice the Lord's first indictment, *"You tolerate that woman Jezebel, who calls herself a prophetess."* Names are powerful, provide identities and often lead to destinies. If this woman lived up to her name, and embraced it's evil past, she chose independence over interdependence. The church is the body of Christ, and therefore, each member connects with others. **[Romans 12:4-5]** Believers lean on fellow believers; no one overcomes individually. True believers enrich their spiritual family through unique callings and giftings. Christians journey together. A non-cohabitant is anti-Jesus.

Jezebel of Thyatira sought preeminence like her predecessors. Anyone who pursues titles (prophetess), or craves recognition, is proud and extremely needy. Almost without exception, self-promoting prophets, like their ancient Thyatiran counterpart, came from dysfunctional broken homes. Since insecure, wounded little boys and girls never received parental validation, especially from a father, they seek approval and recognition from others throughout life. Mix in spirituality and their extreme neediness flares and eventually becomes delusional.

Most of these prophet-types possess a legitimate revelatory gifting(s). God gave each and every believer good gifts. [**1 Corinthians 12**] Since gifts are exactly that, gifts, or grace bestowed upon believers by a loving Father, no one can boast let alone take pride in their abilities. Yet, this is the very thing Jezebel does. She flaunts God-given talents and exalts herself. Jezebel wants followers and preys upon weak, deprived people like herself. But, God opposes the proud. [**James 4:6**]

Like present-day believers, the Thyatirans were enthralled with revelatory powers. Since a Jezebel makes fleeting references to Jesus, her prophesies seemingly originate with God. Right? Hardly. Satan functions supernaturally too, and empowers false prophets. [**Matthew 24:24**] Jesus admonished believers to inspect fruit. [**Matthew 7:16**] Fruit designates species and variety. Real Christians look, act, smell, feel and taste like their Lord and Savior, Jesus. He humbled Himself and always deferred to His heavenly Father. [**Matthew 19:17**] Jezebel doesn't. She's an attention-getter and thrives on personal accolades.

When Jesus judged Jezebel, He challenged the Thyatiran's superficial spirituality. Secret revelations are no substitute for deep, abiding intimacy with Jesus. 'Ooh' and 'ah' experiences carry a believer only so far. Jesus is judgment because light overpowers darkness and the kingdom of God reigns forever. Those who stand with Jesus belong to the kingdom of God, while those who don't remain obedient to dark powers. Although Jezebel feigned godliness, her loyalty resided with Satan. Truth overshadows acceptance, and consequently, tolerance was insufferable for Jesus. Either one sides with the Christ or doesn't. **[Matthew 12:30]**

Jesus charged, *"By her teaching she misleads my servants into sexual immorality and the eating of food sacrificed to idols."* This text baffled me until very recently. Because scripture is truth and transcends the confines of time, this verse should apply to present-day Christendom as well. Scholarship maintains Jezebel taught libertine doctrines or moral permissiveness. I'm sure she did. However, after being exposed to a plethora of Christian ministries throughout the years, I've yet to hear any minister teach on bagging a neighbor's wife, or sleeping with a boyfriend before marriage, regardless of ministerial stream or denominational ties. Nor have ministers endorsed partying or wild celebrations. And yet, sinful human nature endures, including Jezebelian practices. There's nothing new under the sun. **[Ecclesiastes 1:9]** So, what's really going on?

Symmetry earmarks truth. Personal experience must align with truth or scripture. It's similar to saying, 'If the shoe fits, where it.' The shoe represents truth and the foot symbolizes personal experience. Consequently, personal experience must shrink, grow or stay the same in order to properly fit scripture. In the case of Jezebel, my understanding was limited and I grew from it. The primary indictment against the Thyatirans was true then and continues to be true today. But, "it's not what you think it is."

Sexual immorality runs rampant throughout Christendom. Minister's abuse. Adultery and divorce destroy families. Promiscuity plagues youth. Pornography entices and shames. False piety is presently the only distinction between church and world.

However, immorality of any sort is merely fruit and not root. Wicked hearts produce evil. When a believer fully gives his or her heart to anyone other than the Lord Jesus Christ, including prophetic ministers, the willing vessel is committing adultery. **[Revelation 2:22]** Believers are supernaturally married to Jesus. Apparently, a number of the Thyatirans, not all, sought Jezebel over and above the Lord Jesus Christ as their spiritual source and sustenance and entrusted this false prophetess with their hearts. Jezebel usurped Jesus and He was mad. **[Revelation 2:22-23]** Spiritual infidelity produces works of the flesh culminating in sexual immorality.

Sexual immorality obviously occurred in the Thyatiran church. Nevertheless, to simply focus on this aspect of their sinfulness entirely misses the point. This was why Jesus said, *"Then all the churches will know that I am he who searches hearts and minds."* The super-spiritual are extremely elusive and rarely take responsibility for evil intentions. They say things like: 'That's not what I meant.' or 'You can't judge my heart.' or 'You just don't understand.' Perhaps not. However, Jesus judges, and it must be a terrifying experience to hear Him say, *"I never knew you. Away from me, you evildoers!"* **[Matthew 7:23]**

Jezebel was undoubtedly called to the role of prophetess, or at the very least prophetic ministry. Jesus also said, *"From everyone who has been given much, much will be demanded: and from the one who has been entrusted with much, much more will be asked."* **[Luke 12:48]** Certain roles within the body of Christ require more grace than others. Greater callings require greater grace. Prophetic ministry represents one of those roles. So, for Jezebel, or any other minister for that matter, to receive greater grace and use God's goodness for personal ends amounts to serious sin. Even then, Jesus extended mercy to Jezebel by giving her time to repent. What a merciful Lord we serve! She hardened her heart, refused repentance and paid the consequences. **[Revelation 2:21-23]**

Each and every person possesses a deep, burning desire for intimacy that can only be met by God. Whether one recognizes that need or not, it is there. Heartfelt communion is fundamental to humanity. Folks suppress their need by choosing temporal means of fulfillment such as money, food, education, a cause, fame, religion, sex, a career, a spouse, a child and the like. The passionate need for intimacy resurfaces throughout life, and until one wholeheartedly embraces the loving advances of Jesus, he or she will bounce from one worldly fix to the next. Only the love of God offers contentment.

Spiritual elitists thwart intimacy by positioning themselves between God and His beloved children. Jezebel purposely blocks and misleads unsuspecting Christians. Professional clergy, as well as so-called Spirit led ministers, claim special anointings. Rather than directing the spiritually immature to Jesus Christ, these scheming impostors garner personal support and exalt themselves. The super-religious want a kingdom, and in order for their aspirations to be realized, they need followers. The driving force behind the whole wicked enterprise is the spirit of Jezebel. It attempts to usurp the Lord, husbands, God ordained prophets, true spiritual leaders and any other legitimate authority. Jezebel flexes her spiritual muscle to the degree control is exercised over others.

Think about the ramifications. Followings are everywhere: Lutherans follow Martin Luther. Mennonites follow Menno Simons. Others faithfully record Christian programming. Multitudes wait expectantly for papal directives. There are those who belong to prophetic streams and consider Bishop 'so-and-so' the voice of God. Methodists revere John Wesley's legacy. Progressives are members at 'such-and-such' a church. Some chase healing ministries. Many live for the anointed teachings of apostle __. A few attended the Toronto and Brownsville outpourings, and now, the rest of Christendom needs enlightenment. Young boys commit to missions, and suddenly, after a few measly months of service, their church crowns them elders. However, the all-important question is, who's following the Lord Jesus Christ?

Tiny Christian tribes roam the North American spiritual landscape. Exclusivity equals weirdness. Smallness affords tighter control over followers. Unscrupulous leaders trick groupies into believing they've received special revelation from God. In reality, special revelation constitutes satanic secrets. **[Revelation 2:24]** A Jezebelian type prophet views himself as misunderstood, and consequently, rejected by unspiritual Christians. These delusional soothsayers

fashion their ministries after John the Baptist and consider themselves the lone voice of truth crying in the wilderness.

Here are a few examples: A supposedly powerful prayer warrior
spearheads a tight, close-nit band of intercessors who in turn manipulate and coerce a young, insecure pastor into seeing things their
way; Or, an obese prophetess waddles into a Sunday service with her
young protégé and makes sure they're seated up front. She suddenly
begins to shake and quiver during the sermon. The power of God
must be upon her! Next, the messenger of God stands and delivers a
harsh, corrective word to the entire congregation. Even though
Jezebel has absolutely no relationship with anyone there, she's still
going to straighten them all out; Or, the great woman of God coun-
sels broken-hearted parishioners for hours on the phone. She alleg-
edly speaks words of life, but strangely, no one ever heals or matures;
Or, a minister prays 'at' individuals in his fellowship; Or, the itinerant minister always one-ups everyone else; Or, he demands king-like
service instead of serving others; Or, the house prophet gets mad at
the pastor, leaves and takes half the congregation with him; And,
closer to home, the domineering wife barks and belittles her   husband in front of others. These examples represent only a small cross-
section of Jezebelian behavior. Control is always the common de-
nominator. Scary stuff, isn't it?

What does eating food sacrificed to idols mean? Does that entail
eating strangled animals and therefore blood? **[Acts 15:20]** Or,
might the phrase mean exactly that-- eating food sacrificed to idols?
If so, why was this practice so reprehensible for Jesus?

Once again, Jesus' words are timeless. How does the Lord's indictment apply to twenty-first century Christians? Idols are any person, place, or thing that supplants Jesus Christ as Lord and Savior in a believer's heart. This definition is all-inclusive and true. Jesus is Lord! Most believers refuse to acknowledge personal idolatry. The modern mind relegates idolatry to superstitious peoples who bow down before lifeless wood and stone. Ivory-towered notions are just as idolatrous as hard-core materialism.

On a number of occasions, I've heard statements like: 'Lets celebrate our success,' or someone toasts, 'Here's to good fortune.' Others seek 'destiny.' **[Isaiah 65:11]** People honor success above the Lord Jesus Christ. They drink in remembrance of fortune. Destiny promises fulfillment. Each veneration attempts to dethrone Jesus, and as such, constitutes idolatry. The Lord determines the steps of all believers and not fate. **[Proverbs 16:9]** God is the Potter and   Christians are His clay. **[Romans 9:21]** The children of God belong to the kingdom of heaven, and consequently, they are no longer friends with the world. **[1 John 4:4-6]**

The world contaminates the church through destructive ideologies. Friendship with the world represents enmity with God. **[1 John 2:15]** False gods infect unsuspecting believers with deceptive, but gratifying thoughts. **[2 Corinthians 10:5]** Those thoughts form self-serving ideologies. Ideologies find expression through worldly lifestyles. Many western believers unwittingly commit spiritual adultery by worshipping the false gods of success, fortune, and destiny.

Health gurus declare, "You are what you eat." Nutritional science supports this claim. Cheap, fast food diets are incredibly unhealthy and over extended periods of time cause debilitating diseases. Conversely, fresh organic produce devoid of chemical additives is much more nutritious. Folks digest and absorb what they eat. Food consumption affects not only biological functions, but also thought processes and attitudes. Who and what one becomes are inextricably linked to his or her intake.

Professional athletes adhere to planned, strict diets in order to compete at the highest levels. A few resort to illegal steroid use in hopes of gaining an advantage. These cheaters get bigger, stronger and faster than their competitors. The insecure find comfort in sweets, balloon up and insulate themselves from more rejection. Meth addicts deteriorate on the inside and outside. Educated suburbanites stay selective and attempt to make informed, healthy food choices.

If one's food and drink are dedicated to a false god, then it seems the consumer becomes like the deity worshipped. You are what you eat. Christian communion supernaturally affects the believer's spiritual and physical wellbeing. **[1 Corinthians 11:27-32]** A heavenly reality infuses the sacraments. Catholics believe in transubstantiation; that is, during communion, the bread literally turns into Jesus' flesh and the wine into His blood. Satan counterfeits. Are demonic realities invoked during unholy sacraments? Why not? Does the professional athlete look like Jesus, or a comic book hero? Or perhaps an ancient god? Does the obese businessman look like Jesus or pampered gluttony? Does the meth addict look like Jesus or the demoniac? **[Mark 5:1-20]** Does the suburbanite look like Jesus or western success? Are these folks and others inadvertently partaking of food sacrificed to idols?

Food and drink are forms of intimacy. Folks eat with friends and family. Lovers sneak away and enjoy a quiet meal together. Friends share a bottle of wine. Throughout the world, and in all cultures, dinner invitations represent a great honor. It's a subtle way of saying, 'I would like to know you,' or, 'Become a member of my family tonight.'

When believers fail to acknowledge the Lord Jesus Christ, or include Him in their intimate gatherings, they temporarily enter Satan's domain. He destroys and relishes any opportunity to hurt God's chosen ones. A tiny foothold is all Satan requires. **[Ephesians 4:27]** Believers invite unwarranted dangers by excluding Jesus.

Jesus broke bread and passed it to His disciples during the last supper. He said, *"Take and eat; this is my body."* **[Matthew 26:26]** Next, the Lord offered the cup, saying, *"Drink from it, all of you. This is my blood and the covenant, which is poured out for many for the forgiveness of sins."* **[Matthew 26:28]** Since then, Christians the world over, regardless of persuasion, partake of the sacraments in one form or another. Even so, communion is not crackers and little shots of grape juice, but an entire meal as evidenced by scripture. **[1 Corinthians 11:18-34, Jude 12]** Whenever believers come together and eat, whether knowingly or unknowingly, they observe communion. This simple, beautiful Christian practice has been religiously misconstrued and in many ways lost. Many Christians associate communion with somber Sunday morning services once a month.

Others think it involves robe touting clergy hand feeding parishioners after pious incantations. Ultra-spiritual rituals fail to grasp the simplicity of the Gospel.

According to the kingdom narrative, God is Life, and wherever the Lord is, life abundantly overflows. **[John 10:10]** And so, when believers feast in remembrance of the Lord Jesus Christ, they consume pure life. The holy sacraments transcend any and all health secrets: vitamins, Popeye's spinach, green tea, workout routines, honey, cranberry juice, aspirin, colon flushes, organic fruits and vegetables, red wine, antioxidant supplements and anything else. As believers eat Jesus' blood and flesh, they feed from the Tree of Life that renews them physically and spiritually. **[Genesis 3:22]**

However, herein lies the rub. If righteous feasting on the holy sacraments brings health and life, then improper consumption causes sickness and death. **[1 Corinthians 11:30]** Paul said, *"...whoever eats the bread or drinks the wine in an unworthy manner will be guilty of sinning against the body and blood of the Lord."* **[1 Corinthians 11:27]** A number of Corinthians apparently ignored the needs of fellow believers by chowing down and getting drunk during communion. **[1 Corinthians 11:22]** Their love feasts became vile. Self-gratification created divisions. **[1 Corinthians 11:18]**

Institutional Christianity's present understanding of communion is far too narrow. Most ministers interpret the phrase, *in an unworthy manner,* to merely entail unforgiveness towards others or secret sins. It does. But, once again, there's so much more.

Samuel the prophet said, *"For rebellion is like the sin of divination, and arrogance like the evil of idolatry."* **[1 Samuel 15:23]** He coupled arrogance and idolatry. Pride also breeds self-indulgence; 'I want what I want when I want it.' When the three are added together, arrogance plus self-indulgence plus idolatry, an interesting picture emerges. Self-centered people (arrogance) celebrate their passions (self-indulgence), and in the process, step on others. They pursue wants and desires (idolatry) and honestly believe that their fleshly pursuits will ultimately provide lasting happiness and satisfaction. This outline depicts the wretched state of the Corinthians, Thyatirans, and sadly, present day Institutional Christianity.

As already demonstrated, Jezebel was arrogant. She reveled in ungodly passions, pursued supremacy and led others down the path of destruction. **[Revelation 2:20-21]** In all likelihood, Jezebel and her disciples, at one time or another, encountered the Lord Jesus Christ. Nevertheless, wicked desires and demonic influence won them over.

By espousing Jesus as Lord, and hiding under the moniker of Christianity, Jezebel and her groupies placed themselves in a very precarious situation. When the false prophetess and her followers came together and ate food sacrificed to idols, they took Holy Communion in a completely unworthy manner. Paul's warning was reminiscent of Jesus:'

For anyone who eats and drinks without recognizing the body of the Lord eats and drinks judgment on himself. That is why many among you are weak and sick, and a number of you have fallen asleep. But if we judged ourselves, we would not come under judgment. **[1 Corinthians 11:29-31]**

And the Lord's:

So I will cast her on a bed of suffering, and I will make those who commit adultery with her suffer intensely, unless they repent of her ways. I will strike her children dead. **[Revelation 2:22-23]**

In summary, if Jezebel and her Thyatiran' apostates wished to return to the kingdom of darkness, Jesus would oblige them. Love constitutes freedom. God allows folks to choose whomever and whatever they want-- often times to their own demise. Jesus is judgment, and those who stand with Him choose abundant life. But, those who reject Him align themselves with the power of sin and ultimately death. The Thyatirans became presumptuous by taking communion in an unworthy manner. When believers from any dispensation treat Holy Communion with disdain it becomes spiritual and physical poison for them.

One can't help but wonder if this ungodly practice doesn't plague the wellbeing of Institutional Christianity. On any given Sunday, weak and sickly believers fill the pews of churches throughout the western hemisphere. Many take a battery of pills. Others receive weakly treatments. The desperate uproot and chase faith healers.

If Christendom resurrected basic biblical practices, in particular love feasts, just maybe, a number of health issues might suddenly and supernaturally disappear.

Therefore, Jesus presented Himself to the Thyatiran church as the Son of God, and in doing so, summoned heaven's authority. He evaluated their spiritual state. Present-day Institutional Christianity mirrors the Thyatiran church. Jesus commended the Thyatiran's deeds, love and faith, service and perseverance because they were doing more than previously.

Even so, Jesus also brought indictments. The Thyatirans tolerated Jezebel. This woman sought preeminence by referring to herself as a prophetess. Anyone who pursues titles or craves recognition is undoubtedly proud and extremely needy. Most prophet types possess legitimate revelatory giftings. Jezebel wanted attention and flaunted her God-given abilities.

Jesus admonished believers to inspect fruit so that they could identify real from illegitimate. True Christians look, act, smell, feel and taste like Jesus. The Lord challenged the Thyatiran's superficial spirituality by judging Jezebel.

Symmetry earmarks truth. Personal experience must fit scripture.

A number of Thyatirans, not all, looked to Jezebel over and above the Lord Jesus Christ. Sexual immorality is fruit and not root. Wicked hearts produce evil. The super-spiritual are extremely elusive and rarely take responsibility for hidden motives. Jezebel was called to the role of a prophetess, or at the very least, prophetic ministry. However, she hardened her heart, refused repentance and paid the consequences.

Each and every person possesses a deep, burning desire for intimacy that can only be met by God. His love offers true contentment. Spiritual elitists thwart intimacy by positioning themselves between God and His beloved children. Jezebel flexes her spiritual muscle to the degree control is exercised over others. There are followings everywhere, but few follow the Lord Jesus Christ. Tiny Christian tribes roam the North American landscape. Smallness affords tighter control. Special revelation constitutes satanic secrets.

Idols are any person, place, or thing that supplants Jesus Christ as Lord and Savior in a believer's heart. Ivory-towered notions are just as idolatrous as hard-core materialism. The world contaminates the church through destructive ideologies. False gods infect believers with deceptive, yet gratifying thoughts. Believers unwittingly commit spiritual adultery by worshipping the false gods of success, fortune and destiny.

You are what you eat. Who and what one becomes are inextricably linked to intake. Food and drink are forms of intimacy. If one's food and drink are dedicated to a false god, then it seems the consumer becomes like the deity worshipped. Communion is infused with a heavenly reality. Satan counterfeits. Are demonic realities invoked during unholy sacraments? Believers invite unwarranted dangers by excluding Jesus.

The holy sacraments amount to a simple, beautiful meal. According to the kingdom narrative, God is Life, and wherever the Lord is, life abundantly overflows. As believers eat Jesus' blood and flesh, they feed from the Tree of Life that renews them spiritually and physically. If righteous feasting on the sacraments fosters life, then improper consumption causes sickness and death. Institutional Christianity's present understanding of communion is far too narrow.

Arrogance, self-indulgence and idolatry are diabolically tied together. Jezebel and her disciples at one time or another might have possessed a meaningful relationship with Jesus. However, wickedness of heart and demonic influence won them over. They hid under the guise of Christianity and took holy communion in a completely unworthy manner. When believers from any dispensation treat the holy sacraments with disdain, it becomes spiritual and physical poison for them. One can't help but wonder if this ungodly practice doesn't plague the wellbeing of Institutional Christianity. If Christians resurrected basic biblical practices, in particular love feasts, just maybe a number of health issues might suddenly and supernaturally disappear.

THE ANTICHRIST SPIRIT

The contest determines the prize; the greater the contest, the greater the prize. Olympic gold medals are awarded to international winners while state champions receive trophies. Conquering armies loot national treasures while local warlords rule regional tracts.

Jesus pledged,

To him who overcomes and does my will to the end, I will give authority over the nations--He will rule them with an iron sceptor; he will dash them to pieces like pottery--just as I have received authority from my Father. I will also give him the morning star. He who has an ear, let him hear what the Spirit says to the churches. **[Revelation 2:26-29]**

Jesus suddenly shifted His address from the local congregation to the international stage. Why? Does the spirit of Jezebel exercise international authority? Or, is there something even more sinister going on here?

The spiritual warfare crowd has elevated the spirit of control, or Jezebel, to the status she so desires, all-powerful. And, if the truth be told, this wicked spirit acts as a puppeteer behind world leaders and powers. It controls people, groups and even nations. Yet, Jezebel must bow before Jesus Christ and submit to all of His brothers and sisters. No power is greater than Jesus. **[Ephesians 1:19-22]**

Satan's kingdom is divided into a hierarchy or spheres of authority. **[Ephesians 6:12]** Jezebel is a power, but not a principality. Think of spheres of authority in terms of chess. The king represents the most valuable piece on the board, and once he's captured, the game ends. The queen follows in value. Her play, however, is second to none and she moves like all the other pieces combined except the knight. The rook or castle comes next. This piece devastates opponents by sliding vertically and horizontally across the board. The rook also controls lines of play. Bishops move diagonally. Pawns are similar to foot soldiers; marching in step, one space at a time.

Satan challenged the supreme Master, God. The game was over before it began. Satan's king (death) is pinned, and in few short moves, God will checkmate His delusional opponent. **[1 Corinthians 15:54-57]** However, the devil's queen (the antichrist spirit) continues to fly around the board and occasionally captures a godly piece. The rook (the Jezebel spirit) works in conjunction with the queen (the antichrist spirit) by threatening pieces near and far and attempts to dictate battle formations.

Satan's premier principality is the antichrist spirit. It dwarfs all of his other spiritual weapons except death. Wherever someone seeks the limelight, regardless of secular or sacred domains, an antichrist spirit exercises authority. Earthen vessels exalt themselves, and in turn, glorify Satan. This wicked principality shouts, Me! It does everything within its power to trivialize the Person of the Lord Jesus Christ.

Notice what God did and still does: The Father drew attention to His beloved Son. **[Matthew 3:17]** Jesus honored the Father. **[Mark 10:18]** The Lord also testified to the Spirit of truth. **[John 16:7-11]** The Spirit glorified the Son. **[John 16:14]** All deferred to the Other in humility and love.

John challenged fellow believers:

Dear friends, do not believe every spirit, but test the spirits to see whether they are from God, because many false prophets have gone out into the world. This is how you can recognize the Spirit of God: Every spirit that acknowledges that Jesus Christ has come in the flesh is from God, but every spirit that does not acknowledge Jesus is not from God. This is the spirit of the antichrist, which you have heard is coming and even now is already in the world. **[1 John 4:1-3]**

What does test the spirits mean?

Jesus said in the last days folks would run to and fro chasing false christs and false prophets who perform great signs and miracles. **[Matthew 24:23-26]** Originally, I took this passage at face value and felt confused; nobody claimed divinity. I've since revised my initial assessment.

Christ means "anointed one." **[Biblos Matthew 24:23-26]** For years, I've heard the statement, 'He's so anointed.' This expression has become the catchphrase throughout Charismatic circles. Gifted false prophets and false christs love their own press. They revel in personal praise while simultaneously strengthening the rule of an antichrist spirit empowering them. And beware, the anointed ones deliver with astounding revelatory powers and healings.

No one possesses the ability to mask his or her attitude. A person's spirit bleeds through their speech and personality. Attitude is unmistakable and unmasks hidden motives. In this respect, spirit and attitude are interchangeable. Those who garner personal praise and adoration are not serving God, but an antichrist spirit. If a believer merely focuses on signs and wonders, he or she will be in jeopardy of deception. Out of the overflow of the heart the mouth speaks. **[Luke 6:45]** Listen and watch. Who's getting the attention? Who's really being honored? Even the most subtle and sophisticated impersonators can't whitewash self-centeredness. Testing the spirits is a simple, but effective test.

Paul, in his dealing with the Corinthians and the super-apostles battled this very spirit. **[2 Corinthians 11:5]** He detailed their arrogant attitudes, *"When they measure themselves by themselves and compare themselves with themselves, they are not wise."* **[2 Corinthians 10:12]** Conversely, Paul's attitude was, *"Let him who boasts boast in the Lord. For it is not the one who commends himself who is approved, but the one whom the Lord commends."* **[2 Corinthians 10:17-18]** Believers are to know each other by the Spirit and not according to worldly endorsements. **[2 Corinthians 5:16]**

False prophets are mouthpieces for the antichrist spirit. They infect truth with small doses of falsehood. Their prophecies sound super-spiritual and even ring true. Listeners 'ooh' and 'ah.' Christianese sugarcoats deceptive oracles and ignorant believers unequivocally swallow each and every word. If someone has the chutzpah to stand up and blast out a prophecy, then that's good enough for most believers. Personal agendas, then and now, contaminate prophecies. However, regardless of the source, all utterances must be evaluated in light of scripture. The word of God is the one, true guideline for prophetic utterances. Just as the godly practices of communion and testing the spirits were lost somewhere in the archives of Christianity, judging prophecy has been forgotten too. **[1 Corinthians 14:3]**

I used to be avid gun enthusiast and loved long shots. I experienced a profound rush when I hit tiny targets hundreds of yards away. Minor factors at close distances become major factors at great distances: powder, wind, slugs and trigger pull. If I jerked the trigger a little bit on a hundred yard shot, I would still hit the target. However, if I jerked the trigger ever so slightly on three hundred yard plus shots, I missed significantly.

Prophecy is like shooting. A number of factors must be true and synchronized: motivation, purpose, tone and delivery, and most of all, biblical integrity. When these factors become secondary, or in many cases completely ignored, the 'rhema' word misses the mark and misleads unsuspecting believers. With regards to motivation: Is the person motivated by the love of God? Is he stepping out in faith? Or, is he drawing attention to himself? Concerning purpose: Does the word strengthen, encourage or comfort? **[1 Corinthians 14:3]** Or, are people condemned, embarrassed, or perhaps, even shamed? Concerning tone and delivery: Does the vessel demonstrate humility and the kindness of God? Or, does he convey an 'I'm going to fix you' attitude? And finally, regarding biblical integrity: Does the prophecy bear witness with the testimony of the Lord Jesus Christ? **[Revelation 19:10]** Or, does the word glorify someone or something else?

Jesus said, *"I am the way and the truth and the life. No one comes to the Father except through me."* **[John 14:6]** This is the testimony of Jesus. When prophecy lacks these themes--that is, Jesus being the way, the truth, and the life-- or the fleshing out thereof, then the utterance is suspect. The angel of God said, *"For the testimony of Jesus is the spirit of prophecy."* **[Revelation 19:10]** Spirit of God prophecies direct messenger and listener toward the Lord Jesus Christ. Those who glorify Jesus belong to God. **[1 John 5:1]** But, any prophesier who detracts from or diminishes the Lordship of Jesus Christ belongs to an antichrist spirit, and ultimately to Satan himself. **[1 John 4:2-3]**

Jesus promised Himself, the bright Morning Star, to the one who overcomes, and consequently, authority over nations. **[Revelation 2:26, 28]** All things in heaven and on earth are under His Lordship. **[Ephesians 1:20-23]** Jesus prophesied His pledge to the Thyatirans during The Sermon on The Mount. **[Matthew 5:3-10]** He said, *"Blessed are the meek, for they will inherit the earth."* **[Vs. 5]** Meekness is synonymous with humility. Gentleness of heart or humility completely contradicts and opposes the antichrist spirit. Meekness originates with God and accurately depicts the attitude of Christ. **[Philippians 2:5-8]** To the humble in heart, and those who overcome by doing the will of God to the end, they shall inherit the earth and rule nations.

Therefore, the contest determines the prize; the greater the contest, the greater the prize. Jesus promised overcomers in the Thyatiran church authority over nations.

The spirit of Jezebel is a power, but not a principality. Except for death, the antichrist spirit is Satan's premier force. Wherever someone seeks the limelight, regardless of secular or sacred domains, an antichrist spirit exercises authority. Earthen vessels exalt themselves and in turn glorify Satan. An antichrist spirit does everything within its power to trivialize the Lord Jesus Christ.

The Godhead defers One to Another. Believers are to test the spirits. Folks run to and fro chasing false prophets and false christs who perform great signs and wonders. Christ simply means anointed one. No one has the ability to mask his or her attitude. A person's spirit bleeds through their speech and personality. Who's getting the glory?

False prophets are mouthpieces for the antichrist spirit. They sugarcoat their prophecies with Christianese. Judging prophecies, like communion and testing the spirits, has been lost in the archives of Christianity. A number of factors must be true and synchronized when judging prophecy: motivation, purpose, tone and delivery, and most importantly, biblical integrity. *"For the testimony of Jesus is the spirit of prophecy."* He is the way, the truth, and the life.

Jesus prophesied His pledge to the Thyatirans during The Sermon on The Mount. The meek, or the overcomers, inherit the earth and rule nations.

CLOSING REMARKS

The unseen realm is real. Spiritual bullies torment lost humanity and pick on unsuspecting believers. The spirit of Jezebel casts her spells wherever someone controls another person(s), from individual families to heads of state. Control is the antithesis of love, and therefore, has no place in the kingdom of God. Satan controls, but God is Love.

When a spiritual component is incorporated, as in the case of Christianity, control is strengthened and becomes even more deceptive. Wicked hearts agree with devilish spirits. Professional clergy, empowered by the spirit of Jezebel, arrogantly position themselves between God's chosen vessels and the Lord Himself. Rather than acting as guides for needy souls, Christian pundits cultivate patronage hoping to capture the hearts and minds of followers and thereby establishing their own kingdoms. Spellbound leaders elevate themselves to a place reserved solely for the Lord Jesus Christ. The spiritual blockade results in spiritual immorality and all manner of fleshly pursuits.

The antichrist spirit uses control or the spirit of Jezebel for its purposes. Gifted, but self-serving anointed ones perform as puppets for this wicked principality. They control followings, and in so doing, detract from Jesus. The antichrist spirit forever attempts to diminish the Lordship of Jesus--the one, true Christ.

Money

*"Those who set out to serve both God and Mammon soon discover
that there is no God."*
LOGAN PEARSALL SMITH

The ancient, sacred cow of money is well fed and fat. Money presides over the pantheon of gods. Institutional Christianity began worshipping Mammon over a thousand years ago. Today, more than ever, Christians emulate this false god. Parishioners sport crosses around their necks and rearview mirrors, but their hearts are stamped with dollar signs. Money exercises authority each and every Sunday over churches throughout the West, and really the world. Only the love of God trumps Mammon's seductive powers.

This chapter begins by highlighting the intimate relationship between religion and money. Next, two very important questions are posed to all Christians. I then address the misuse of New Testament verses by money disciples. I also expose the misconstrued doctrine of Abraham's blessings. Later, Paul's reference to ministerial compensation receives clarification. A brief exposition of true riches follows, and lastly, personal experiences and concluding remarks close the chapter.

A very important principle is as follows: The nearer one draws to God the less concerned he or she is with money. Conversely, the further one drifts from God the more concerned he or she is with money.

Once again, the Lord said:

I tell you the truth, the Son can do nothing by himself; he can do only what he sees his Father doing, because whatever the Father does the Son also does. For the Father loves the Son and shows him all he does. **[John 5:19-20]**

Observance requires proximity. Jesus and the Father are One. **[John 10:30]** Remember, the closer one draws to God the less concerned he or she is with money. The glory of God overshadows all other riches. Consequently, Jesus despised earthly riches.

The Lord rebuked the religious leaders:

Woe to you, blind guides! You say, If anyone swears by the temple, it means nothing: but if anyone swears by the gold of the temple, he is bound by his oath. You blind fools! Which is greater: the gold, or the temple that makes the gold sacred? You also say, If anyone swears by the alter, it means nothing; but if anyone swears by the gift on it, he is bound by his oath. You blind men! Which is greater: the gift, or the alter that makes the gift sacred? **[Matthew 23:16-19]**

Those indictments were biting and harsh. However, all are true. Jesus took the Pharisees to task. They loved money more than God.

The parable of The Rich Man and Lazarus is found in **Luke 16:19-31**. A rich man lived in luxury while a beggar named Lazarus lay at his gate, suffering daily. At death, the rich man went to hell and Lazarus to Abraham's bosom. The rich man begged father Abraham for relief and asked him to send Lazarus to warn his brothers. Abraham replied that if his brothers paid no attention to Moses and the Prophets, then they wouldn't listen to someone raised from the dead.

A friend of mine highlighted an interesting detail, which I consistently read over, and somehow, missed. **[Tackett] Verse 19** says the rich man wore purple and fine linen. These garments were reserved for priests. **[Exodus 28:6]** The rich man was a spiritual leader! Priests came from priestly families, and therefore, the rich man's brothers were expected to know the Holy Scriptures too. Yet, when a person truly knows something, he or she becomes accountable for that understanding. This entire, self-centered family disregarded the Holy Scriptures and neglected the poor. **[Jeremiah 22:16-17]**

Has religion changed? Someone recently informed me of a minister making well over two hundred thousand dollars a year. Another popular church pays their pastoral staff in excess of six million dollars annually for services rendered. These figures aren't unusual. American religion is peppered with money stories. Ministry became a lucrative vocation. And yet, an eerie and alarming similarity exists between Jesus' parable and present day Institutional Christianity.

Another disturbing development of the prosperity doctrine is the notion that God's favor equals riches and disfavor poverty. Ok... Jesus said:

If the world hates you, keep in mind that it hated me first. If you belonged to the world, it would love you as its own. As it is, you do not belong to the world, but I have chosen you out of the world. That is why the world hates you. Remember the words I spoke to you: No servant is greater than his master. If they persecuted me, they will persecute you also. **[John 15:18-20]**

According to Jesus, almost without exception, earthly riches translate into friendship with the world. And so, favor with God implies enmity with the world, especially religion. Earthly rulers love money because it undergirds their authority and control.

John the apostle amplified the Lord's teaching:

Do not love the world or anything in the world. If anyone loves the world, the love of the Father is not in him. For everything in the world--the cravings of sinful man, the lust of his eyes and the boasting of what he has and does--comes not from the Father but from the world. **[1 John 2:15-16]**

Shear, outright hostility exists between the kingdom of God and the world.

TWO IMPORTANT QUESTIONS

Here are two very important questions every Christian must ask himself or herself: One; Did Jesus ever speak positively of money? And two; Did He ever ask for money? The answer to each question is absolutely no!

Then, why does money play such a vital role in churches and ministries today? Each and every Sunday the spiel goes like this: 'It's now time to bring the tithes and offerings to the Lord. He loves a cheerful giver.' At this point, the rising superstar sings a solo. The televangelist's shtick is slightly different: 'If you believe in this ministry, then we need your help. We are now broadcasting throughout Africa (or Asia) with the Gospel of Jesus Christ. Help us take the word of God to the lost.' During the entire shtick, sick and dying refugees flash across the screen.

Christians must also ask themselves: Why didn't Jesus plead and whine for money? Do Christians define Christ, or does Christ define Christians?

Others argue, 'That was then and this is now. We live in a world where we need more resources.' Is that so? Modern cultures possess conveniences, resources and opportunities that the ancients couldn't fathom. The average American lives better than kings and queens in biblical times, or for that matter, a little over a hundred years ago. Be honest.

Financial planners are modern day church prophets. They use **Matthew 25:14-30**, or The Parable of the Talents, as their scriptural reference. Good Christians are good stewards. Churches host week-long stewardship drives and the prophets prophesy. The new sooth-sayers detail techniques and strategies for generating money and keeping it. In response, the average parishioner gets excited, tips God, and builds a future nest egg.

John 12:1-6 is a fascinating passage. Mary poured a pint of very expensive perfume over Jesus' feet and wiped them off with her hair. **[Vs.3]** Judas Iscariot (the betrayer) became angry and said, *"Why wasn't this perfume sold and the money given to the poor? It was worth a year's wage."* **[Vs.5]** Judas' ulterior motives triggered his super-spiritual question and comment. **[Vs.6]** He attempted to manipulate Jesus by appealing to the Lord's ministry practices. This passage demonstrates that Jesus gave His money to the poor. The Lord also fed thousands with leftovers. **[Mark 6:32-44, 8:1-10]** Not bad for a homeless man. **[Matthew 8:20]**

The disciples learned their lesson. **Acts 2:44-45** says, *"All the believers had everything in common. Selling their possessions and goods, they gave to anyone as he had need."* Shortly thereafter, Peter and John went to the temple for prayer and encountered a beggar. Peter made a remarkable statement, *"Silver or gold I do not have, but what I have I give to you."* **[Acts 3:6]** Evidently, Peter wasn't using believer's offerings for personal gain.

Paul implored fellow believers on rare occasions. **[1 Corinthians 16:1-4, 2 Corinthians 8:1-15]** Nevertheless, his requests were always on behalf of needy brethren.

MISUSE OF NEW TESTAMENT VERSES

Like all scripture, one can easily twist the Gospels:

For everyone who has will be given more, and he will have abundance. **[Matthew 25:29]**

Give and it will be given to you. A good measure, pressed down, and shaken together and running over, will be poured into your lap. For with the measure you use, it will be measured to you. **[Luke 6:38]**

Still other seed fell on good soil. It came up and yielded a crop, a hundred times more than was sown. **[Luke 8:8]**

And

I tell you, use worldly wealth to gain friends for yourselves, so that when it is gone, you will be welcomed into eternal dwellings. **[Luke 16:9]**

These scriptural one-hit-wonders are repeatedly spun in support of greed.

Matthew 25:29 belongs to the passage of Matthew **25:14-30**. The master entrusts his servants with talents according to their abilities. **[Matthew 25:15]** The master's business becomes the good servant's business. One ceases ministering the moment he or she focuses on personal gain. Genuine concern for others is at the heart of service.

Love binds together any healthy relationship: whether master/servant, father/daughter, or employer/employee. A relationship is doomed once it collapses into a 'What do I get out of it' attitude by either party. All good gifts come from the Father and He freely gives. **[Matthew 7:11]** God is good, always. The child of God utilizes his or her gifts to the best of their ability.

Love is the impetus behind freedom. Healthy, secure people are at liberty to take risks and accept challenges. Regardless of success or failure, the beloved is forever loved. Therefore, the child of God steps out in faith and aggressively pursues the Father's concerns.

However, the wicked servant doesn't love. He is concerned about his wellbeing. **[Matthew 25:24-26]** The wicked servant is an illegitimate child who never knew the Father, or belonged to the family of God. If this person loved, then he wouldn't be afraid. **[Matthew 25:25, 1 John 4:16-18]**

Thus, **Matthew 25:29** and The Parable of the Talents **[Matthew 25:14-30]** has absolutely nothing to do with wealth acquisition. Rather, the thrust of the passage illuminates the loving relationship between the Father and His children.

Luke 6:38 represents another money anthem. Get-rich Christians believe, 'If I give to others, then I'm going to get something in return and preferably more.' In a warped, roundabout way, generosity is a means to an end, money. The greedy use giving to pull strings and manipulate. Manipulation is a subtle, indirect form of control, and control is witchcraft. Witches practice witchcraft.

A witch is a person who attempts to control people or situations through spiritual and natural channels in hopes of satisfying carnal desires. Contrary to popular myths, most witches aren't cape wearing, toothless old hags. No, many are beautiful, articulate people living respectable lives. Institutional Christianity is chock-full of them. Witches scheme and manipulate through various devices. Some whine. Pretty ones seduce. Mean ones intimidate. Many flatter. Most brag. All lie-- especially to themselves. And yes, there are those who purposely conjure up spirits.

The greedy use **Luke 6:38** as a spell. Since the word of God is living and active, soothsayers chant **Luke 6:38**, and with any luck, their If/Then proposition yields dividends. **[Hebrews 4:12]** Like Balaam, lustful hearts are blinded by personal ambition. **[Numbers 22-24]** Money hungry Christians honestly believe God endorses avarice.

Luke 6:38 is found within the context of **Luke 6:27-42**. This entire passage is a blueprint for godly conduct. Jesus begins the passage with, *"Love your enemies…"* **[Luke 6:27]** He went on to say: *"And if you lend to those from whom you expect repayment, what credit it that to you? …But love your enemies, do good to them, and lend to them without expecting to get anything back. Then your reward will be great, and you will be sons of the Most High, because he is kind to the* *ungrateful and wicked. Be merciful, just as your Father is merciful."* **[Luke 6:34-36]**

Charity, by its very nature, gives and asks nothing in return, even from enemies. **[1 Corinthians 13:5]** God's children exhibit His love. Businessmen pursue profit, but the godly freely give. The Father is raising sons and daughters and not moneychangers.

Jesus also said not to judge or condemn, but to forgive. **[Luke 6:37]** These secondary commandments flesh out the golden rule, *"Love your neighbor as yourself."* **[Matthew 22:39]** Heart condition determines attitude. True believers bless others without personal compensation. The children of God derive their satisfaction and fulfillment from pleasing God.

Charitable giving is the polar opposite of monetary reward. To maintain **Luke 6:38** infers financial gain is to utterly reject the Gospel.

Prosperity doctrines exploit **Luke 8:8** and incorporate the principle of sowing and reaping. The contrived reasoning is as follows: By sowing wheat, one reaps wheat. Likewise, if one sows money, he or she reaps money. Good ground yields greater returns. Consequently, money sowed in fertile ground produces a bountiful harvest.

What is good ground? According to prosperity advocates it's them! Worldly riches require wealth acquisition. The greedy induce money by sermonizing prosperity. Scandalous ministers disguise ungodly desires with stories of starving children, Bibles for pagans and upcoming outreaches. They lie to themselves and others.

Luke 8:8 can only be understood in the context of **Luke 8:5-15**, or The Parable of the Sower. Jesus provided the correct interpretation, *"But the seed on good soil stands for those with a noble and good heart, who hear the word, retain it, and by persevering produce a crop."* **[Luke 8:15]** A noble and good heart is not a money field.

Money lovers distort **Luke 16:9** as well. Supposedly, God wants believers to be rich in order to bless others. But that's not what scripture teaches. Rather, Jesus was saying, 'Give your earthly belongings away.' The Lord elaborated,

"Do not store up for yourselves treasures on earth, where moth and rust destroy, and where thieves break in and steal. But store up for yourselves treasures in heaven, where moth and rust do not destroy, and where thieves do not break in and steal. For where your treasure is, there your heart will be also." **[Matthew 6:19-21]**

One restrains heavenly resources by hoarding temporal goods. **[Luke 16:10]**   Gold and silver fail God's criteria for true riches. **[Luke 16:11]** Jesus depicted worldly treasures as detestable in God's sight. **[Luke 16:15]**

The greedy spin other New Testament verses too. A favorite is **3 John 2**,

Dear friend, I pray that you may enjoy good health and that all may go well with you, even as your soul is getting along well.

Supposedly, as one thinks correctly, he or she prospers physically and financially. This prosperity tenet completely contradicts **1 John 2:15-16**. Most importantly, though, it violates Jesus' teaching.

First consider the health issue. Jesus walked in divine health. The Lord never struggled physically. People were healed and restored wherever He went. So, is there biblical precedence for divine health? Absolutely.

Nevertheless, I have a major reservation concerning the health gospel. Many folks battle physical conditions, and often times, their condition is extremely debilitating or even life threatening. Consequently, health disciples consistently condemn and shame those who struggle. Callous and trite comments are made: 'Be it unto your faith,' or 'You need more faith,' or 'You have sin in your life,' or they may ask 'Are you confessing your healing?' All this sounds well and good, and on certain occasions may prove true. However, Jesus always ministered out of love and compassion. At the beginning of his ministry, He quoted Isaiah by saying, *"He has sent me to proclaim freedom for the prisoners and recovery of sight for the blind, to release the oppressed, to proclaim the year of the Lord's favor."* **[Luke 4:18-19]** That quote radically diverges from the previous religious babble.

A beautiful story is found in **Luke 7:11-16**. As Jesus entered a community, He encountered a funeral procession. A widow lost her only son. **Verse 13** says, *"When the Lord saw her, his heart went out to her and he said, don't cry."* Jesus laid His hand on the coffin and raised the young man back to life. **[Vs. 15]**

Scripture is silent concerning the deceased's life. He might have been the worst sinner in the entire community, and because of his wretched lifestyle, died. But, that's not the point. Jesus, moved by love and compassion, resurrected the boy and returned him to his grieving mother.

Jesus healed an invalid by the pool of Bethesda. **[John 5:1-15]** Later, the Lord found the man and said, *"See, you are well again. Stop sinning or something worse may happen to you."* **[John 5:14]** Jesus did not embarrass or shame him. No one will ever know, for all of eternity, what sin(s) he committed. Jesus freed a prisoner from the power of sin.

Whether one is an advocate of health and wealth, is not, or somewhere in between, love and compassion remains the only standard for ministry. There is no place in the kingdom of God for mean spirited comments towards the brokenhearted and oppressed. Truth becomes error and right is wrong when divorced from love. Jesus said, *"For by your words you will be acquitted, and by your words you will be condemned."* **[Matthew 12:37]**

What about money and **3 John 2**? For real estate, the theme is-- Location, Location, Location! For scripture, the theme is--Context, Context, Context! Rather than plucking a verse from scripture and twisting the meaning, consider the entire passage:

To my dear friend Gaius, whom I love in the truth.

Dear friend, I pray that you may enjoy good health and that all may go well with you, even as your soul is getting along well. It gave me great joy to have some brothers come and tell about your faithfulness to the truth and how you continue to walk in the truth. I have no greater joy than to hear that my children are walking in the truth. **[3 John 1-4]**

John used the term truth four times. Gaius was a Roman name, and in all likelihood, this person was a gentile convert. Gaius left the world for the kingdom of God. As a believer in Jesus Christ or the

Truth, he stood in complete opposition to the standards and values of the world. Selfishness, or worldly thinking, incites lusts for temporal pleasures. **[James 4:1-4]** According to the Truth, however, one was to even love his or her enemies, bless them and wholeheartedly pursue the kingdom of God. **[Luke 6:27, 14:26-27, 14:33]** Moreover, with his constant reference to truth, John was probably combating Gnosticism; a cultic heresy denying the incarnation of Christ.

This passage never alludes to money. It implies just the opposite. The trappings of the world no longer entangled Gaius because he knew the truth, or the Lord Jesus Christ. **[John 1:14]** The passage continues:

Dear friend, you are faithful in what you are doing for the brothers, even though they are strangers to you. They have told the church about your love. You will do well to send them on their way worthy of God. **[3 John 5-6]**

Whether Gaius possessed little or much, he generously gave. When one belongs to the world, he or she wants. Selfishness seeks personal wellbeing. Conversely, when one belongs to the Lord, he or she gives. Love seeks the wellbeing of others. The real meaning of the verse quickly reveals itself with contextual reading.

Another pet verse is **2 Corinthians 8:9**. It says,

For you know the grace of our Lord Jesus Christ, that though he was rich, yet for your sakes he became poor, so that you through his poverty might become rich.

The English word rich is translated from the Greek word plooteho, which means wealth or material belongings. **[Biblos 2 Corinthians 8:9]** So, at face value, one immediately infers Jesus made Christians wealthy. He did. With the coming of Christ, and His death and resurrection, believers are adopted into God's royal family. **[John 17:20-26, Galatians 4:6-7]** Believers are joint heirs with Christ and therefore entitled to all the resources of heaven. **[John 16:23-24, Ephesians 2:19-22]** The faithful are no longer restricted by earthly limitations. Rather, the heavenly Father unconditionally loves His children and meets all their needs without reservation. **[John 14:23, Luke 12:7, Matthew 6:30]**

Then-- Why is Institutional Christianity fixated on money? Ministers whine and beg for financial help. Something is horribly wrong with Institutional Christianity's present practices.

The answer is two-fold and straightforward. Jesus said:

"So do not worry, saying What shall we eat? or What shall we drink? or What shall we wear? For the pagans run after all these things, and your heavenly Father knows that you need them. But seek first his kingdom, and his righteousness, and all these things will be given to you as well." **[Matthew 6:31-33]**

Jesus promised that the heavenly Father would meet all of one's needs. Believers are blessed. They're fantastically rich! However, Jesus also told believers to seek first the kingdom of God, His righteousness and everything else would follow. **[Vs. 33]** Isn't that interesting? Institutional Christianity hasn't pursued God's kingdom or His righteousness. These money chasers resemble pagans. The greedy depend upon their talents, gifts, hustle and even scams for wellbeing.

Secondly, the money chasers attempted to establish personal empires. Religion masqueraded under the guise of Christianity for financial gain. If Institutional Christianity referred to itself as a business, no issue would exist. Businesses are designed to generate money. Christians, however, who possess the Spirit of Christ, are life givers and not takers. **[John 14:16]** Believers rely upon their heavenly Father for material needs and everything else.

Reconsider **2 Corinthians 8:9**. And, like **3 John 2**, read in context. At the beginning of chapter 8 it says:

And now, brothers, we want you to know about the grace that God has given the Macedonian churches. Out of the most severe trial, their overflowing joy and their extreme poverty welled up in rich generosity. For I testify that they gave as much as they were able, and even beyond their ability. Entirely on their own they urgently pleaded with us for the privilege of sharing in this service to the saints. **[2 Corinthians 8:1-4]**

The Macedonians were utterly poor by worldly standards. Conversely, according to heaven, they were fantastically rich. The Macedonians freely and joyfully gave. They considered giving a privilege and an honor. God provided regardless of their sacrifice.

Paul, in **2 Corinthians 8**, challenged the Corinthian church to imitate the Macedonians and generously give to needy brothers and sisters. It's practically inconceivable how a person might twist this passage to mean, 'I'm entitled to money.' Paul shatters the money mantra a couple of verses later:

For if the willingness is there, the gift is acceptable according to what one has, not according to what he does not have. Our desire is not that others might be relieved while you are hard pressed, but that there might be equality. At the present time your plenty will supply

what they need, so that in turn their plenty will supply what you need.
[2 Corinthians 8:12-14]

Believers are prosperous despite worldly circumstances. The heavenly Father lovingly provides for all. A situation may require a little and another abundance. Perhaps a brother needs encouragement while a neighbor needs food. Jesus spoke words of life, fed the hungry and paid His taxes. **[John 4:21-24, 6:1-15, Matthew 17:24-27]** There was always enough. The Father richly blesses His children so that they may be generous on every occasion.

Jesus offers the best illustration of wealth:

As he looked up, Jesus saw the rich putting their gifts into the temple treasury. He also saw a poor widow put in two very small copper coins. I tell you the truth, he said, this poor widow has put in more than all the others. All these people gave their gifts out of their wealth; but she out of her poverty put in all she had to live on. **[Luke 21:1-4]**

Who's really wealthy?

ABRAHAM'S BLESSINGS

Abraham's blessings are another leg on the sacred cow of money. **Galatians 3:14 & 29** says:

He redeemed us in order that the blessing given to Abraham might come to the Gentiles through Christ Jesus, so that by faith we might receive the promise of the Spirit.

And

If you belong to Christ, then you are Abraham's seed, and heirs according to the promise.

Prosperity doctrine correctly maintains God richly blessed father Abraham. A lengthy list of blessings is found in **Deuteronomy 28**. Christians are grafted into God's family through faith in Jesus Christ. **[Romans 11:17]** Consequently, believers are entitled to Abraham's blessings.

I'm all for blessings. The Father's goodness rained down on me: I have a beautiful wife and son; We're healthy; We have a roof over our heads and the refrigerator is full; We have friends; Family loves us; Even strangers show us kindness; Our car runs well; We live in one of the most beautiful places on earth; I'm educated; We play and we travel. Oh, believe me, I understand blessings.

However, there are two serious issues pertaining to this leg of the prosperity doctrine. The blessings found in **Deuteronomy 28** were given to Moses on behalf of the Israelites and conditional. If the Israelites carefully obeyed God, they enjoyed blessings. **[Deuteronomy 28:1-2]** Disobedience brought curses. **[Deuteronomy 28:15]** Blessings and curses are understood only in conjunction with the law. After the death and resurrection of the Lord Jesus Christ, God sent His Holy Spirit. Through the sanctifying work of Christ, true believers are no longer under the law, but rather, live in grace and transcend stringent guidelines. What the faithful were once powerless to do, they can now do through the empowerment of the Holy Spirit. The Father changes hearts.

Here is a classic example of majoring on the minors. The greedy see through the lust of their hearts, claim to be Abraham's decedents, and then demand material blessings from God. They want frosting and forget cake. Once again, blessings are wonderful.

However, what's truly amazing is God gave His very Spirit to all who call Jesus Lord and Savior. God never leaves nor forsakes His children. How, and I emphasize how, can anything compare? Jesus said of the patriarch, *"Your father Abraham rejoiced at the thought of seeing my day; he saw it and was glad."* **[John 8:56]** What believers enjoy and often take for granted, unabated intimacy with God, Abraham longed for, but never realized.

Institutional Christianity, which includes High Church, Evangelicals, Charismatics and the Conference Circuit, all look like the god they worship, money. North American religion is monetarily super rich. How many businesses are able to open a couple of times a week and continue paying exuberant bills and staffing costs? I'm not aware of any. Even McDonalds and Wal-Mart would go broke. If ministries across North America tallied their tithes and offerings for a couple of months, the gross would undoubtedly exceed developing nations total GNP.

Clergy selection is determined by degrees and wage negotiation rather than trials and tribulations. Professionals mirror money. Christianity adopted worldly values and became a rich man's religion. The poor are pitied. If an impoverished person shows up at church, God forbid, the rich swoop down on the wayward sinner and hopefully convert him.

Greed infected the ancients too:

You say I am rich: I have acquired wealth and do not need a thing. But you do not realize that you are wretched, pitiful, poor, blind, and naked. I counsel you to buy from me gold refined in the fire, so you can become rich; and white clothes to wear, so you can cover your shameful nakedness; and salve to put on your eyes so you can see...Those whom I love I rebuke and discipline. So be earnest and repent. **[Revelation 3:17-19]**

Notice the last verse. Regardless of one's causefusion and idolatry, both then and now, Jesus unconditionally loves.

Three legs were chopped off the money cow. The god of this age tipped over and fell. The money doctrines dismally fail when held up to the life and teachings of the Lord Jesus Christ. Each self-serving tenet was exposed and shown for what it truly represents, a lie. Behind each lie lurked greed or the love of money.

MINISTERIAL COMPENSATION

What about **1Timothy 5:17-18**? Paul says,

The elders who direct the affairs of the church well are worthy of double honor, especially those whose work is preaching and teaching. For the scripture says, Do not muzzle the ox while it is treading out the grain, and the worker deserves his wages.

In other words, one who preaches the Gospel deserves compensation for his or her services. Paul actually made reference to Jesus' teachings. When the Lord sent out the seventy-two, He gave them specific instructions:

When you enter a house, first say, Peace to this house. If a man of peace is there, your peace will rest on him; if not, it will return to you. Stay in that house, eating and drinking whatever they give you; for the worker deserves his wages. Do not move around from house to house. **[Luke 10:5-7]**

Eating, drinking and sleeping constitute necessities of life, regardless of race, gender or age. Jesus demonstrated from this passage that ministers of the Gospel should receive material blessings for their efforts. If one constantly grapples to secure basic necessities, it becomes very difficult to do anything else, even for God. But, to spin **1 Timothy 5:17-18**, and infer Jesus endorses financial gain for ministry is equally absurd.

TRUE RICHES

One golden leg remains and there's a very good reason; God is golden and rich, and He extravagantly blesses His children materially, spiritually and in every other way. His favor and goodness rests upon those who call Jesus Lord and Savior and even upon those who don't. Yes, that's right. His loving kindness extends to all! Christians serve a Father who never leaves nor disowns. His love endures forever. Ultimately, divine Love transcends understanding. Believers live the most amazing lives ever imagined by communing with their Father. It's true. I testify. I wouldn't trade my relationship with the Lord for anything or anyone.

PERSONAL EXPERIENCES

Sometime ago, a friend told me about a church that regularly experienced signs and wonders. I listened and kept my mouth shut. Unbeknownst to her, I visited this church two times and left appalled. The apostle, as the faithful call him, spent no less than twenty to thirty minutes asking for and extolling the virtues of money.

Signs and wonders are no guarantee of God. Ignorant believers become spellbound, and shortly thereafter, they're duped. While in their trance, mesmerized followers shelve their Bibles, and without reservation, accept each and every lie. Powers and principalities perform miraculous signs through false christs and false prophets.

On another occasion, I attended a seminar. Here, the so-called prophet stood before paying customers, me included, and shouted, "I've got the anointing, and you don't! And that's why you're here." Customers were shocked. His arrogance resurfaced throughout. He was rude and unkind to a number of individuals. This obese show-man wore something like loose fitting, silky purple pajamas. Even draped, his demeanor exuded sensuality. Supposedly, if a person purchased one of his CD sets for a meager seventy dollars, he or she received deeper revelation.

My examples are bizarre, but true. Each story highlights extrem-ism. And yet, when held up to scripture, Institutional Christianity's practices are no less extreme or bizarre. The pressuring, whining, bullying and manipulating are detestable in God's sight. Since when did real ambassadors of the Lord Jesus Christ require money for acts of service? I can't find any biblical precedence. Occasionally, as mentioned previously, an offering was taken on behalf of needy believers. In fact, false prophets sought gain while true prophets refused payouts. **[Numbers 22:31-34, Jude 11, 2 Kings 5:15-27]**

CONCLUDING REMARKS

Over the years, I've read countless Christian books. Many authors place sweet, flowery prayers at the end of their chapters. Sorry, I won't. If greed overtook you, ask for forgiveness and repent. The Father loves unconditionally and welcomes you open armed.

Power

"Nearly all men can stand adversity, but if you want to test a man's character, give him power."
ABRAHAM LINCOLN

Power is the matriarch of sacred cows. Money is a means, but power is an end. Money undergirds, but power makes the rules. Those who wield power dominate others. Satan's carnal kingdom covets power.

In this chapter, I uncover Institutional Christianity's use of image, elitism and titles. Hypocrisy gets exposed as well. I unravel four widespread demonic doctrines. The bondage created by rules, requirements and fear is detailed. I also explain the fear of God. Additionally, I describe God's power.

IMAGE, ELITISM, AND TITLES

In **Matthew 23** Jesus exposed the deceitful practices of the Pharisees. He said to His disciples and the people:

Everything they do is for men to see. They make their phylacteries wide and the tassels on their garments long; they love the place of honor at banquets and the most important seats in the synagogues; they love to be greeted in the marketplaces and to have men call them Rabbi. But you are not to be called Rabbi, for you have only one Master and you are all brothers. And do not call anyone on earth father, for you have one father, and he is in heaven. Nor are you to be called teacher, for you have one Teacher, the Christ. The greatest among you will be your servant. For whoever exalts himself will be humbled, and whoever humbles himself will be exalted. **[Matthew 23:5-12]**

The very first thing to notice is Jesus' indictment against the religious leader's motivation, *"Everything they do is for men to see."* Power brokers, driven by selfish and lustful hearts, then and now, seek personal recognition. In Jesus' day, these posers wore accentuated religious ornaments; phylacteries were small boxes that contained revered scriptures, and tassels were knotted extensions of prayer shawls. Yet, Jesus said the Pharisees' phylacteries and tassels were exaggerated or wider and longer than customary. These hypocrites wanted attention and spotlighted their spirituality in order to exult themselves. Now, before chuckling and saying, 'silly Pharisees,' consider Institutional Christianity's practices.

High church officials flaunt gowns and robes fit for a king. What kind of image does that project? Obviously, they consider themselves special or above common folk; rich, ornate attire reinforces elitism. However, elitism is not confined to the ritualistic, but poisons every segment of institutionalism. I've visited the church of the new suit too. Here, supposedly, Sunday is the high-holy-day and the faithful must look their very best. But I thought the Sabbath was made for man? **[Mark 2:27]** And then there are the enlightened ones who claim a 'no dress code.' Their mantra goes, 'We come as we are.' Yet, the lead pastor dons Calvin Klein cool and struts up and down the stage like a peacock. His wife is a Cosmo girl and looks suburban hip. Although his staff and inner circle adopt a 'come as you' are policy, strangely, they all dress exactly like the pastor and his wife.

There's a spiritual twist to the children's story, The King's New Clothes.

Jesus went on to charge these professionals with garnering honor and positions of prominence both in the community and in the synagogues, all-the-while relishing their titles. The pattern is easily discernible--elitism. In order for the ambitious to achieve and maintain power, they must be perceived as special and distinct. Earlier, the sacred cow of money was exposed; wealth is highly valued among the religious, and often viewed as an endorsement by God in the eyes of the naïve and ignorant. However, an even more diabolical tactic is spiritual elitism. Professionals separate themselves from others so that they can control and dominate commoners. These elitists deceive others into believing they've achieved a super-spiritual state of being. Embellishment and exaggeration are well-used tools. Eventually, commoners give up or they grind out their faith striving for unattainable realities and standards.

As Jesus alluded to, titles are an integral part of hypocrisy. **[Matthew 23:13, 15]** Holy huddles gather and crown each other with honorary ranks like apostle, prophet, evangelist, pastor and teacher. The majority of these folks are tormented with the little man's disease, inferiority. In turn, they spread inferiority by making others feel second-class too.

The institution of high church uses a different set of titles, but no less exclusive: father, priest, vicar, bishop, archbishop, metropolitans, primates and cardinals. Believe it or not, this is not an exhaustive list. Generally, high church places a greater premium on degrees and intellectualism than do other streams, and so, their hierarchal structure is even more convoluted.

Yet, Jesus admonished His disciples not to accept titles or award prestigious designations to others. Why? The disciples were brothers or family because of their relationship with Jesus, and consequently, sons of the Most High God. **[John 15:1-17, Romans 8:17]** Furthermore, a gifted leader does not lord over others, exact homage or require special treatment. Just the opposite! Leaders serve others, regardless of relationship. Jesus said, *"The greatest among you will be your servant."* **[Matthew 23:11]**

DOCTRINE OF DEMONS

Time and again, Jesus referred to the religious elite as hypocrites. **[Matthew 23:13, 15, 23, 25, 27, 29]** Paul encountered the same opposition, and reinforced Jesus' teachings:

The Spirit clearly says that in later times some will abandon the faith and follow deceiving spirits and things taught by demons. Such teachings come through hypocritical liars, whose consciences have been seared as with a hot iron. They forbid people to marry and order them to abstain from certain foods which God created to be received with thanksgiving by those who believe and who know the truth. **[1 Timothy 4:1-3]**

This passage has been referred to as The Doctrine of Demons. Most readers converge on the satanic teachings of 'don't marry' and 'don't eat.' However, a couple of underlying principles is submerged in this text and pertains directly to the discussion.

Paul, like Jesus, described these perpetrators of deceit as hypocrites. Notice where the hypocritical liars received their instruction from--demons! Did Jesus' religious adversaries receive their doctrines from the devil? Absolutely. **[John 8:44]** Has Institutional Christianity circulated demonic lies? For sure.

What is a hypocrite? Most people immediately categorize drug addicts, alcoholics, thieves, perverts and the like into the broad class of hypocrisy. However wrong and destructive their lifestyles are to themselves and others they fail hypocrisy on critical points. Do habitual sinners lie? Absolutely. A drug addict will lie and steal from his own family. Do they conceal their sin? Yes. Perverts are ashamed of their sexual practices and appetites. Yet, if these habitual sinners aren't inebriated or hustling, more than not, they confess and denounce their failures when pressed. Most are horrified to think that their family members or children might end up like themselves. To categorize these broken people who battle habitual sins as hypocrites is wrong and completely mistaken. If anything, the sordid reality is another indictment against Institutional Christianity. While leadership has sought prestige and self-exaltation, they've been powerless to free the captives.

According to Jesus, hypocrisy is composed of superficial religiosity. Hypocrites want to appear holy and righteous before others. Image is extremely important to them. If their image is tainted or devalued, and others view them less than favorably, then their preeminence is compromised. This is why professionals demand titles, special seating and recognition from others.

The motivation behind image is pride or superiority, and therefore sin. And who is the force behind sin? Satan. If one is under the authority of the devil, he or she receives lies from him. Satan's kingdom is not divided, and so, his religious cohorts are not about to help the captives. **[Matthew 12:25-29]** Hypocrisy is sin wrapped up in a self-righteous form of godliness that seeks the praise of men over the approval of God. These folks do the right things for all the wrong reasons.

For decades, high profile ministers have fallen. I feel sorry for them. Even more so than dishonest politicians, the liberal media takes great delight and pleasure in defrocking holier-than-thou clergy. Nevertheless, Jesus made it very clear what would happen, *"For whoever exalts himself will be humbled…"* These gifted, but self-serving ministers exalted themselves. Jesus also said, *"For he who is least among you all--he is the greatest."* **[Luke 9:48]** And, once again, Paul expounded on Jesus teachings:

Do nothing out of selfish ambition or vain conceit, but in humility consider others better than yourselves. Each of you should not only look to your own interests, but also the interests of others. Your attitude should be the same as that of Christ Jesus… **[Philippians 2:3-5]**

How many believers really consider others better than themselves? A very convicting question isn't it?

What about Ananias and Sapphira? Over the last couple of years, I've heard a number of prophecies forecasting the return of the days of Ananias and Sapphira. **[Acts 5:1-11]** Their story goes like this: Ananias and his wife Sapphira sold a piece of property and lied about the price. **[Vs. 1 & 8]** They laid a portion, but not all of the money at the apostles' feet. **[Vs. 2]** Peter supernaturally exposed their lie and said, *"You have not lied to men but to God."* **[Vs. 4]** Ananias dropped dead, and then shortly thereafter, Sapphira fell dead too. **[Vs. 5 & 10]**

God's judgment seemed harsh. Ananias and Sapphira gave some of their money to the church, right? Who hasn't fudged a little or cut a corner now and then? What's the big deal?

Our confusion stems from perspectives. If one takes a human or worldly perspective, he or she can quickly dismiss the Spirit's dealings with the husband and wife duo as unfair and over-reactive. However, that assessment is an oversimplification and incorrect. Generally, humankind majors on God's minors, and conversely, God's majors are humankind's minors.

For millennia, God watched the devil and sin ravage His beloved creation. And for millennia, the Father shielded and protected His children. Eventually, He died for all of creation in the person of the Lord Jesus Christ, and thereby freed humanity from the dominion of Satan and the bondages of sin. Then, Ananias and Sapphira came along, claimed to be God's own, and took the very thing that cost Jesus His life and blood, sin, and wrapped it up as godly. Talk about a slap in the face. This was exactly what the Pharisees did, as well as many present-day religious leaders; they take sin, disguise it and declare holy. The essence of any satanic enterprise is self-interest, and consequently, self-promotion. Above all else, hypocrites want to look good before others. Image is vital, because, like money, proper appearance undergirds worldly power. Hypocrites relegate God to a cursory role or completely disregard Him.

If one peruses scripture, he or she will find other hypocrites. Re-member, hypocrisy is sin wrapped up in a self-righteous form of godliness that seeks the praise of men over the approval of God. The life of king Saul is a classic example. He was head and shoulders above everyone else in Israel. **[1 Samuel 9:2]** Saul valiantly fought Israel's enemies. **[1 Samuel 11:1-11]** Later, however, he became special in his own eyes. **[1 Samuel 15:12, 17]** Rather than following the instructions of the Lord, Saul acted in self-interest and sought the approval of men. **[1 Samuel 15:1-3, 20-21, 24]** Like Ananias and Sapphira, Saul was hypocritical.

Are there other examples? Certainly. Cain was self-centered. **[Genesis 4:1-12]** The deaths of Nadab and Abihu are examples. **[Leviticus 10:1-3]** Eli could be classified here. **[1 Samuel 2:27-29]** Absalom was hypocritical. **[2 Samuel 15:1-12]** Job's three self-righteous friends disgusted God too. **[Job 42:7-9]** Even Peter fell into delusion. **[Galatians 2:11-13]** If God despises anything, it's hypocrisy.

Spiritual leaders maintain that Christianity is ultimately a matter of obedience to God. Scripture certainly supports that contention. **[John 14:15]** Yet, throughout scripture I can also find a plethora of examples, one after another, of God's children disobeying, and often times, their waywardness demonstrated sheer evil. **[2 Samuel 11]** No, there is a much deeper issue here.

Once again, pride ignites hypocrisy. Self-exaltation hardens the heart, and eventually calcifies the human spirit thereby making it impervious to the promptings and influence of the Holy Spirit. The core of hypocrisy is a deceitful, rigid heart. The self-serving seek preeminence at the price of their neighbor's welfare. If the hypocrite doesn't love their neighbor, then he or she certainly doesn't love God. **[1 John 4:20]** Jesus' rebuke was timeless:

Woe to you, teachers of the law and Pharisees, you hypocrites! You are like whitewashed tombs, which look beautiful on the outside but on the inside are full of dead men's bones and everything unclean. In the same way, on the outside you appear righteous but on the inside you are full of hypocrisy and wickedness. **[Matthew 23:27-28]**

Understand, every saint stumbles or falls at one time or another. **[1 John 1:8]** Thus, every believer has been disobedient. However, the humble heart is transparent and flexible because it is filled with the love of God. The believer quickest to repent is also the one who walks in the greatest humility. A kind, tender heart is the surest indication of love, and consequently, the presence of God.

Earlier, I stated that there were other principles submerged in the text. The unbiblical, but perennial doctrine of 'Who's Your Covering?' continues to deceive. A variation of this demonic doctrine is 'You have to come under authority in order to have authority.' Sometimes the lie is spun this way, 'Who's your pastor?' or 'What church do you belong to?' Each question is designed to force believers under the rule of pseudo-spiritual authorities. Most of those who press the issue are attempting to create their own fiefdom, or expressed in modern vernacular, ministry.

Once again, Jesus forbade believers to call one another master, father, or even teacher. Undoubtedly, Jesus was anti-title, and therefore, the title pastor is no less a misnomer. Scripture refers to one Good Shepherd and that is Jesus. **[John 10:11-16]**

Because true believers are connected to the Head, the Lord Jesus Christ, many of them operate and function as apostles, prophets, evangelists, pastors and teachers. **[Colossians 1:18, Ephesians 4:11-13]** However, to pay homage to these gifted believers, or elevate them above others, is   contrary to scripture and even flows from an antichrist spirit. Didn't Jesus say all believers were brothers and therefore family? An antichrist spirit draws attention to its host and contradicts the very nature and attitude of Jesus. If a minister or ministry constantly subjects one to arrogance, judgment, heavy-handed demands and remarks, rudeness, criticism, boasting, brazen-ness, crassness, or a know-it-all attitude, then leave. What is the Spirit of the living Christ like? Jesus said:

Come to me, all you who are weary and burdened, and I will give you rest. Take my yoke upon you and learn from me, for I am gentle and humble in heart, and you will find rest for your souls. For my yoke is easy and my burden is light. **[Matthew 11:28-30]**

The church question is equally bizarre. Why are there so many fellowships and denominations? According to scripture there is one church and this living, breathing entity represents the body of the Lord Jesus Christ. **[John 15:1-17 and 1 Corinthians 12:12-13]** The church is not a Sunday morning gathering or a denominational rally. No, the body of Christ is a real, organic being attached to the Head, Jesus. If one does not belong to Jesus Christ and possess His Spirit, then he or she is not a member of the church. **[Romans 8:9]** Simple! What does it really mean to be Baptist, Mennonite, Catholic, Pente-costal, Nondenominational, Anglican, Charismatic, Lutheran, Vine-yard, Presbyterian, Unity, Orthodox, Methodist, and on and on?

I don't know. Understand too, there are literally hundreds, if not thousands of subgroups within these larger sets. So, are these folks disciples of Jesus? Or, are they followers of a dead, revered saint? Without judging and knowing individual hearts, the latter is a much more plausible explanation.

Many will undoubtedly counter that diversity is one of the surest indicators of God's presence. **[1 Corinthians 12:14-31]** This is not diversity but pettiness. Aside from a few isolated instances, these groups are elitist and self-promoting. They highlight a minor truth, or whatever their shtick may be, while ignoring the Truth, Jesus Christ, who commanded believers to love one another. **[John 15:17]**

And still others will accuse me of doing the very same thing I'm criticizing-- being elitist. Let me address that accusation.

Another segment of Christendom considers themselves cutting-edge and free. Instead of committing to long-standing traditional organizations, these enlightened ones have joined movements: third wave, healing, renewal, revival, prophetic, spiritual warfare, inner healing, conferences, simple church and even house church. Over the last few years I've been an advocate of house church. As of late, however, I'm forced to reevaluate my views and convictions. I am not a member of any movement. I belong to my Lord and Savior, Jesus Christ. After digging through scripture, and doing extensive reading, I continue to believe that house church or small intimate groups of one kind or another are the purest form of Christianity. Only in close, transparent loving relationships have I or any believer for that matter grown. Yet, to place house church as the spiritual pinnacle of Christianity is wrong. Although house church is probably the most biblical model, it nevertheless constitutes a medium and not the finisher of my faith, the Lord Jesus Christ. As I reflect over the years, intimate gatherings have refreshed and furthered me in my journey. Even so, these stops along the way are watering holes at best and not my home.

Few people grasp or understand authority. Ministers who play the authority card are generally vying for position and power. Their rhetoric stems from self-serving agendas and ideologies. These professionals want one's submission and obedience in order for their passions to be realized. The ultra-spiritual framing for personal agendas is vision. Supposedly, just like Moses' encounter on Mount Sinai **[Exodus 31:18]**, the man or woman of God receives a vision directly from heaven which he or she then casts before the commoners. The vision must be carried out because it's the will of God. Interestingly enough, most of these visions promote and elevate the visionary. After all, they're the chosen ones and know best.

Authority is the power to enforce values. Authority comes from who one is or the entity being represented. Once again, a crude but simple example is the school bully. A young tough's authority comes from himself or the gang he represents. His subjects are afraid of physical harm. At one time or another, he's most likely carried out one of his many threats. The bully is extremely self-centered, and younger, smaller children cower to him.

With this thought in mind, consider modern day ministry practices. Is the minister who flashes the authority card concerned for fellow believers, or, like the school bully, promoting self? When a ministry emphasizes authority over and above relationship they're probably promoting themselves. If one doesn't submit to their God ordained vision and terms, then the believer is out of the will of God and in jeopardy of missing their destiny or worse. Personal exaltation was never a value of Jesus.

James and John competed for position in the kingdom of God through their mother's request. **[Matthew 20:20-23]** The other disciples became angry, and Jesus set them all straight:

You know that the rulers of the Gentiles lord it over them, and their high officials exercise authority over them. Not so with you. Instead, whoever wants to become great among you must be your servant, and whoever wants to be first must be your slave--just as the Son of Man did not come to be served, but to serve, and to give his life as a ransom for many. **[Matthew 20:25-28]**

If Christians take Jesus at His word, then they are not to rule or exercise authority over one another. As the head of the spiritual family, this role is reserved for the Lord Jesus Christ. If anything, Jesus challenges believers to serve and lay down their lives for others just as He did.

The advocates of proper authority regularly cite The Faith of the Centurion. **[Matthew 8:5-13]** According to their doctrine and interpretation of the story, the centurion received his blessing because he submitted to authority and understood proper alignment. **[Vs. 8-9]** However, as I stated earlier, few understand authority. Once again, authority stems from who one is, and in most cases, who is being represented. In the case of Jesus, He was and is the only begotten Son of God, and as such, the one true Representative of the Father. **[John 3:16, Hebrews 1:3]** That's authority. The Lord's teachings and signs and wonders exhibited authority from above. Scripture says, *"… the crowds were amazed at his teaching, because he taught as one who had authority, and not as their teachers of the law."* **[Matthew 7:28-29]** A believer must ask himself a simple, but very important question, Why did the centurion seek Jesus and not a Roman official or Pharisee? He understood authority! Caesar and his armies backed Roman officials. The Pharisees and teachers of the law represented themselves. How could any of these so-called authorities heal the centurion's sick, dying servant? They couldn't. In the final analysis, both groups were pawns for Satan. **[Matthew 4:8]** Conversely, Jesus represented God as revealed by His life and values. Rest assured, the centurion witnessed firsthand Jesus' teachings and miracles, or, at the very least, he heard about them from a reliable source. Why else would he seek Jesus?

If someone demands submission, or in a subtle, roundabout way maneuvers for allegiance, then the believer could very well be entertaining a messenger of Satan.

Perhaps the silliest ploy of all is the laughable doctrine of 'Who's Your Covering?' The doctrine essentially maintains that commoners need spiritual protection, and since a special saint has ascended to a higher level, he or she shields fellow believers from the wiles of the enemy as they come under his or her superior authority. How absurd!

Jesus said after His death and resurrection:

All authority in heaven and on earth has been given to me. **[Matthew 28:18]**

And Paul said:

And God raised us up with Christ and seated us with him in the heavenly realms in Christ Jesus in order that in the coming ages he might show the incomparable riches of his grace, expressed in his kindness to us in Christ Jesus. **[Ephesians 2:6-7]**

Lastly:

For in Christ all the fullness of the Deity lives in bodily form, and you have been given fullness in Christ, who is the head over every power and authority. **[Colossians 2:9-10]**

And so, believers are seated in the heavenly realms with Christ, and filled with His very presence. Moreover, every power that exists, both in heaven and on earth are subject to the Lordship of Jesus. Now, if this is true, then what does any real believer in Christ need protection from? Is some evil power going to bully Jesus? Or, does Jesus need a spiritual covering too? Each believer is a joint heir with Jesus Christ, and therefore, walks in His authority and power. **[Galatians 3:26-29, 1 John 2:6]**   Paul had a very appropriate warning for believers:

"See to it that no one takes you captive through hollow and deceptive philosophy, which depends on human tradition and the basic principles of this world rather than on Christ." **[Colossians 2:8]**

RULES, REQUIREMENTS, AND FEAR

The power brokers employ another sneaky tactic in their game plan--rules and requirements. If one is constantly jumping through hoops and attempting to fulfill the elitist's requirements for godliness, he or she can never enter into intimacy with God. False expectations cause busyness, and busyness detracts from intimacy with our Father and spiritual family. Often times, their ruse sounds something like this: 'If you were really committed...' or 'We need someone to...' or 'Before you can do this, you must...' As long as one is running to and fro, he or she is under the control of the religious elite. It's the proverbial hamster and wheel story; one frantically runs as fast as he or she can and goes nowhere.

Jesus went right to the heart of the matter:

Woe to you, teachers of the law and Pharisees, you hypocrites! You shut the kingdom of heaven in men's faces. You yourselves do not enter, nor will you let those enter who are trying to. **[Matthew 23:13-14]**

And:

Woe to you, teachers of the law and Pharisees, you hypocrites! You give a tenth of your spices-- mint, dill and cumin. But you have neglected the more important matters of the law--justice, mercy and faithfulness. You should have practiced the latter, without neglecting the former. You blind guides! You strain out a gnat but swallow a camel. **[Matthew 23:23-24]**

The elitists functioned as a hindrance, rather than as a guide for those desiring to know God. Their religious traditions obstructed instead of assisting. They stressed trivia and ignored the spirit of the law: justice, mercy and faithfulness. While yoking others with unreasonable and unsustainable loads, they became harsh and demanding. **[Matthew 23:4]**

When one merely focuses on trivia and details, he or she inevitably forgets purpose. As stated earlier, the law was good because a kind and loving Father instituted it in order to protect and help His children. Love initiated the law, and love fulfilled the law in the person of the Lord Jesus Christ. **[Matthew 5:17]** This is why Jesus said the greatest commandments were to love God with all of one's being, and the other like it, love your neighbor as yourself. **[Mark 12:30-31]** When love is the standard, rules and regulations become meaningless. However, only through the transformative work of the Holy Spirit can a person be changed from a lawbreaker into a child of God. **[2 Thessalonians 2:13-17]**

As I've stated in previous writings, the more rules and regulations there are, the less of God there is. Prisons are the epitome of ungodly institutions. The governing authorities determine every moment and detail of a prisoner's life. In the same vein, Institutional Christianity heaps requirements upon ignorant and unsuspecting believers. For example, I've heard this one, 'After you complete our five week discipleship class, you can become a member of our church and pray for others. You'll even get a certificate.' Really! I've yet to find that requirement in scripture. To this very day, others go so far as to tell folks whom they can and can't marry, as well as what foods are acceptable and unacceptable. Again, I'm not embellishing. Paul referred to these controlling doctrines as demonically inspired and the proponents thereof as hypocritical liars. **[1Timothy 4:1-3]**

The motivation behind rules and requirements, and consequently every religious system, is fear. Fear drives people. Fear forces folks to show up Sunday after Sunday so that they don't forsake the gathering of saints, regardless of the strain on their families. Fear pushes the recovering addict to meetings. Fear compels the guilt-ridden

Sunday school teacher to remain faithful. Fear requires the committed to sit through another boring program. Fear drags the intercessor to powerless prayer meetings. Fear persuades the loyal to shake hands and smile one more Sunday.

If a carpenter's primary tool is a hammer, then Institutional Christianity's tool of choice is fear. This diabolical tactic is perhaps most readily used in sermons. Hypocritical ministers threaten and coerce folks into compliance. These fear mongers convince the naïve and unsuspecting that God is going to get them, or worse yet, He'll throw them into hell unless of course they worship Him and start volunteering at church. There's a deal.

In general, the justification for utilizing fear goes like this: God will use whatever means necessary to keep people out of hell. But, as I stated earlier, God does not fight fire with fire. Satan murders to achieve his desired ends. Should God murder too? Satan destroys. Should God destroy lives for the greater good? When one steps back and considers the ramifications, it's completely absurd. Try finding fear in The Sermon on the Mount. **[Matthew 5:3-10]** That message of good news and hope was preached to a dying and perishing people. God has never stooped to the devil's level, nor will Satan ever rise to the Father's stature.

Fear, and all its attributes, has absolutely, irrevocably no place in the kingdom of God. No one can snatch a believer away from the love of God. **[John 10:29]** A son is always a son, and always will be.

Scripture also says:

God is love… There is no fear in love. But perfect love drives out fear, because fear has to do with punishment. The one who fears is not made perfect in love. **[1 John 4:16, 18]**

Many will argue that I'm ignoring large portions of scripture. What about Paul's divine conversion? Wasn't he scared? Or, Explain **Isaiah 11:2** and the fear of the Lord? And, Doesn't **Proverbs 1:7** say that the fear of the Lord is the beginning of wisdom?

Paul, prior to his conversion, lived in fear. A whole, healthy person doesn't go around killing folks or imprisoning them. **[Acts 8:1]** Broken, fearful people hurt and attack others. When Paul encountered the risen Lord on the road to Damascus, he was left speechless. **[Acts 9:7]** Since God is perfect Love and pure Light, He stands in complete opposition to Satan, his subjects and the kingdom of darkness. **[John 1:4-5, 1 John 4:16]** Whatever is hidden in one's heart gets immediately exposed before the presence of the Lord. Was Paul terrified? Without a doubt! But understand, at that moment Paul was still a child of darkness and fear consumed him. Paul was transformed after his conversion, and instead of fear leaving him speechless, he went on to write two of the most beautiful passages in the entire Bible, **Romans 8 and 1 Corinthians 13**. Fear hides, but love is transparent and confident. Fear distorts and creates confusion. Love, however, sees best and desires to know and be known. **[1 Corinthians 13:12]** Since the death and resurrection of the Lord Jesus Christ, every believer can go boldly and confidently before the throne of grace because they have entered into a loving, familial relationship with the Father. **[Hebrews 4:16]** As Paul said, *"For you* *did not receive a spirit that makes you a slave again to fear, but you received the Spirit of sonship."* **[Romans 8:15]**

Proverbs 1:7 and **Isaiah 11:2** both refer to the fear of the Lord. Words often lose meaning and substance when translated into another language. Here, our English word fear fails to encompass and fully appreciate the meaning behind the Hebrew word yirah. **[Biblos Proverbs 1:7, Isaiah 11:2]** Other meanings include: morally, reverence, dreadful and exceedingly. If one embraces the fuller meaning, then fear seems entirely inadequate, especially as one reads scripture through the lens of the Lord Jesus Christ. The Lord is my Father, and yet, He absolutely transcends me in every imaginable way. With this thought in mind, it would be far more appropriate to refer to the exceedingly, dreadful reverence of the Lord, rather than the fear of the Lord. Fear has to do with punishment, but love honors, respects and reveres. He's my Father and He's my God. Unless a believer walks in the love of God, he or she continues to view the Lord from a distorted, skewed understanding and misrepresent Him. Remember, the exceedingly, dreadful reverence of the Lord is the beginning of knowledge. **[Proverbs 1:7]**

Jesus said:

I tell you the truth, everyone who sins is a slave to sin. Now a slave has no permanent place in the family, but a son belongs to it forever. So, if the Son sets you free, you will be free indeed. **[John 8:34-36]**

And so, for myself, and every other believer who calls Jesus Lord and Savior we are free! I am not required to do this or that, or fulfill any other obligation except to love the Lord my God with all my being and my neighbor as myself. Moreover, all things are permissible for me, but not all things are beneficial. **[1 Corinthians 10:23]** I have the freedom and liberty to do as I please as long as I take into consideration the welfare of others. I'm equally irritated when I hear, 'don't do this' and 'don't do that.' I cringe. It's like hearing fingernails on a chalkboard. I've submitted myself to the yoke of the Lord Jesus Christ and to Him alone. His yoke is light and easy because love rules in the kingdom of God. Reread the Gospels and count the Lord's 'don'ts.' This undertaking is as empty and futile as my other challenges. Why? Jesus brought freedom and not restriction. **[2 Corinthians 3:17]** Only in reference to the religious leaders and their practices did Jesus caution and warn His disciples. **[Matthew 16:5-12]**

Obviously, those who feel threatened will accuse me of rebellion. Absolutely not! But, I am opposed to biblical myths. Scripture is very clear:

Obey your leaders and submit to their authority. They keep watch over you as men who must give an account. Obey them so their work will be a joy, not a burden, for that would be of no advantage of to you. **[Hebrews 13:17]**

However, notice the reference to authority. Again, authority is the power to enforce values and stems from who one is or the one being represented. Remember the centurion? He and others were responsive to Jesus' authority because His teachings and miracles revealed who the Lord was, and who He represented, the Father. Unless believers are treated with humility and love, or the values of heaven, one must question a so-called leader's authority. True representatives or ambassadors of the Lord Jesus Christ consistently mirror His Personhood. If a so-called leader doesn't bear the fruit of the Spirit, and therefore the character of Jesus, the believer is under no obligation to cow-tail to selfish wishes and desires.

The second sentence says, *"They keep watch over you as men who must give an account."* When one watches over someone else, he or she is protecting him or her, and has his or her best interest in mind. The leader is not garnering support, demanding allegiance or service or loading the believer down with unnecessary burdens. If anything, the leader is guiding his or her fellow believers into a deeper relationship with the Father.

Scripture also clearly states, *"Submit to one another out of reverence for Christ."* **[Ephesians 5:21]** Relationships between believers are a two-way street, whether one leads or not. Those who know Jesus recognize His voice. As a result, a believer readily submits to the voice of the Lord when God speaks through brothers and sisters of the faith. Discipleship goes back and forth. No one in the kingdom of God is to rule or lord over another. Even the Lord referred to His disciples as friends. **[John 15:15]** Friendship alludes to equality. In the case of Christianity, believers are family and Jesus represents the first born of many. The Lord Jesus Christ is at one and the same time God and big Brother. Consequently, regardless of one's role and function, believers are to respect and honor each other.

GOD'S POWER

Like material wealth, God grants power. Believers were created to exercise God given authority. Within every person is an innate hunger and desire for power. And so, how one satisfies or addresses that need is of the greatest importance. As demonstrated, Satan is the author of illegitimate power. Throughout the ages, the devil used religious leaders to enslave people and continues to do so. Conversely, legitimate power flows from the presence of God. [Acts 1:8] Only in an intimate, personal relationship with the Lord Jesus Christ is authentic power awarded via His Spirit. In turn, the Spirit of Christ transforms the believer, who then affects everyone and everything around him or her. Believers are light to a dark and perishing world. They carry the glory of God.

Believers are to walk as Jesus did. [1 John 2:6] Jesus loved, and walked in the greatest of humility. Jesus healed. [Matthew 8:2-4] Jesus raised the dead. [John 11:1-44] Jesus exercised authority over nature. [Mark 4:37-41] Jesus transcended physical laws. [Luke 9:12-17] Jesus supernaturally spoke into people's lives. Jesus taught. [John 4:7-42] Jesus chased away demons. [Matthew 17:14-18] These are the Lord's ways and standards and not the exception. [John 14:12] It constitutes the power of God. And, the power of God is to be a living reality for each and every believer.

CONCLUDING COMMENTS

Once again, I'm not going to ask believers to recite a nice religious prayer. If I described your situation in the preceding pages, and you've been under satanic control, walk away. God will lead you to like-minded believers. Pray that God will open the eyes and ears of your former oppressors to the Christ.

Success

"You have reached the pinnacle of success as soon as you become uninterested in money, compliments, or publicity."
THOMAS WOLFE

If money and power are revered sacred cows, then success is the offspring. The three are inextricably bound together. Power invariably sets goals of control for itself, and therefore, numbers are the surest indication of success' health and wellbeing; how many people showed up, and how much money came in. The mindset believes that more people translate into more money. I've known a couple of ministers who skillfully played the game. One pastor in particular zeroed in on the wealthy, and made sure he personally wined and dined them. If one wasn't wealthy or beautiful, the commoner was assigned to the care of an underling. His manipulative, yet sophisticated maneuvering funded church enterprises.

Institutional Christianity's definition of success is the notion that more people equals more money. Here's the proof. Try a simple experiment. Ask a faithful churchgoer, 'How's church going?' Almost without exception, he or she will respond according to numbers: 'We were packed.' or 'There were a lot of visitors.' or 'We've been averaging well over three hundred people every Sunday.' If the churchgoer belongs to the inner circle, the conversation gravitates towards money: 'We're close to paying off the sanctuary.' or

'The tithes are down this month.' or 'We still need to raise another ten thousand dollars for our mission's trip.' Try my experiment.

In the ensuing pages, I expose two heartbreaking issues plaguing Christendom. I then discuss the notion of more people in relation to worldly success. Next, true success is revealed. I also highlight the importance of overcoming.

TWO HEARTBREAKING ISSUES

Over the last couple of years, I've encountered an interesting, but explainable paradox. Thus far, no one has really challenged my reasoning. In other words, unless people are just trying to be kind, which I'm sure many are, most folks agree with my contentions. And yet, very few believers are able to free themselves from religious trappings. Why? There are two very disheartening reasons.

Regardless of one's vocation, he or she possesses convictions. For example, an athlete may need to improve her stamina. Yet, to get up an hour earlier every day and run forty-five minutes requires a great deal of focus and dedication. Or, maybe a couple wants to tour Italy. A budget is set, and all frills and extras get nixed: movies, dinner-dates, weekend trips and more. Is the training and delayed gratification worth the extra effort? For a handful of people, yes it is. But, for the vast majority of folks, the sacrifice often proves too great.

The same reasoning applies to Institutional Christianity. A number of so-called believers readily recognize the discrepancies between scripture and present day Institutional Christianity. However, to buck the satanic system and walk away necessitates immense courage. Smug, religious mockery awaits the brave. Even family members turn on their own flesh and blood and brand them cultic. If an ethnic component is mixed in, the condemnation becomes especially mean-spirited and isolating. The Truth costs.

The Jews wrestled with this very issue during Jesus' day; the approval of God or the praise of men. Scripture says in reference to Jesus:

Yet at the same time many even among the leaders believed in him. But because of the Pharisees they would not confess their faith for fear they would be put out of the synagogue; for they loved praise from men more than praise from God. **[John 12:42-43]**

People hide in the crowd. It's easier to go with the clique than to be honest and biblical. Of course, many so-called Christians say they believe in Christ and choose to worship God conventionally. And that's fine. Nevertheless, if one's going to be biblically honest, most long-standing church traditions and more recent religious practices are contrived as this book attempts to demonstrate. Be honest. An unredeemed human condition keeps most people fear bound and crowd captive. Who doesn't want acceptance? However, whose acceptance are Christians really after? Scripture is clear, *"Fear of man will prove to be a snare, but whoever trusts in the Lord is kept safe."* **[Proverbs 29:25]**

The second proposition is even more disturbing. The confession of the overwhelming majority of Christians lacks substance. They have no intimate relationship with the Lord Jesus Christ.

A favorite saying among a few believers, myself included, is, *For those who have eyes to see and ears to hear.* This figure of speech is drawn together from different texts. **Mark 4:11-12** says:

…The secret of the Kingdom of God has been given to you. But to those on the outside everything is said in parables so that, they may be ever seeing but never perceiving, and ever hearing but never understanding; otherwise they might turn and be forgiven!

And:

…For judgment I have come into this world, so that the blind will see and those who see will become blind. **[John 9:39]**

These verses imply that a small number of believers recognize the Truth. Or, as others and myself like to say, *For those who have eyes to see and ears to hear.*

Why then do some perceive the workings of God and understand His scriptures, while others remain blind and ignorant? Only by the grace of God is anyone capable of knowing the Truth. **[1 John 4:19]** The Spirit of Christ relentlessly pursues and influences humankind. However, the self-righteous, religious, self-centered, arrogant, hard-hearted, wealthy, famous, beautiful, positioned, successful (worldly), self-reliant, stiff-necked, hateful, educated, and unforgiving often resist and ignore the tender advances of the Holy Spirit. Now, before my words become misconstrued, and folks accuse me of saying that wealth, beauty, education, fame and position are evil things in and of themselves, I'm not. But, if these prospects become idolatrous, and cause a person to become self-absorbed and resistant to God's kindness, then yes these things are harmful. From what I've witnessed throughout the years, the downtrodden and brokenhearted are much more receptive to the advances of God.

Jesus said:

I praise you Father, Lord of heaven and earth, because you have hidden these things from the wise and learned, and revealed them to little children. Yes, Father, for this was your good pleasure. **[Matthew 11:25-26]**

If one doesn't have the Spirit of Christ residing in their life, then he or she is not a Christian. **[Romans 8:9]** Scripture appears dark and mysterious to professing, but Spirit-less Christians. Spiritual truths are spiritually discerned and require the illumination of the Holy Spirit. **[1 Corinthians 2:14]** The Spirit of God leads authentic believers into all truth. **[John 16:13]**

Here's more proof. Sunday after Sunday, Spirit-less parishioners experience Spirit-less preaching at their Spirit-less church. For the vast majority, this weekly ritual amounts to their only spiritual nourishment-- sort of. Once again, these so-called Christians possess no intimate relationship with the Lord Jesus Christ. They continue insisting upon religious intermediaries rather than going directly to the throne of God. And, more often than not, these religious intermediaries fail to receive their revelation from the heart of God as well, but instead they too subsist on a parasitic faith. Most pastors are well versed in pretend Christianity, pop-psychology, stuffy commentaries and current fads. Ear-tickling entertainment substitutes for Spirit-led ministry.

After a person has encountered the living Christ, nothing else satisfies. The believer becomes lovesick, and he or she desires God, alone. Because the Spirit of the living Christ resides in the believer, she is never separated from God and communes with Him day and night, and even in sleep. The Father's revelations are overwhelming and life changing. After experiencing tender, intimate conversations with God, slick well-rehearsed sermons feel like a complete waste of time, and most are. How does anything compare to spending time alone with God? John the apostle understood this. He said:

As for you, the anointing you received from him remains in you, and you do not need anyone to teach you. But as his anointing teaches you about all things and as that anointing is real, not counterfeit-- just as it has taught you, remain in him. **[1 John 2:27]**

MORE PEOPLE

Since the sacred cow of money has already been slaughtered, let's revisit Institutional Christianity's first all-important component of success-- more people. Is there biblical precedence for multitudes in the life and ministry of Jesus? Without question! On one occasion, Jesus ministered in a home and there was such a large crowd that four men tore a hole in the roof so that their paralyzed friend could be lowered down to Him. **[Mark 2:1-5]** More than once, Jesus miraculously fed thousands. **[Matthew 14:15-21, Mark 8:1-9]** He ministered to an entire town of Samaritans. **[John 4:27-42]** Massive throngs surrounded Him on a number of different occasions. **[Luke 8:40-45]** Clearly then, 'more people' has the semblance of biblical merit.

Yet, as I read the Gospels, Jesus seemed just as concerned if not more so for the individual. Jesus loved Lazarus, and raised him back to life. **[John 11:1-44]** He showed mercy to a leper. **[Matthew 8:1-4]** The Lord ministered to Peter's mother-in-law. **[Mark 1:29-31]** He healed a crippled woman. **[Luke 13:10-13]** Even a child received Jesus' touch. **[Matthew 17:14-19]** Each and every crowd was comprised of needy individuals seeking the Lord's intervention.

Think about this too: Did Jesus ever intentionally pursue the multitudes? Did He and His disciples target and canvas certain towns? Was success even a value or a consideration for Him?

Jesus never once pursued the multitudes or attempted to attract more people, but rather, the crowds chased Him. **[Matthew 14:34-36]** If anything, scripture demonstrates that Jesus squelched fan-fare and popularity. **[Luke 5:14]** The Lord regularly lost disciples instead of increasing His following. **[John 6:53-66]** Planned strategies and targeted communities are the tactics of modern day marketers. Conversely, the Lord Jesus Christ was Spirit-led, and therefore, spontaneously responded to the will of His Father. **[John 3:8, 34]**

Success, then, when defined by numbers whether in terms of money or people had no meaning whatsoever for Jesus. So, is success even worth considering? Yes, it is. The real problem lies in Institutional Christianity's worldly bias.

TRUE SUCCESS

So, what is success? Is it winning the championship game? Ascending to national office? Having your own brand? Rising to international notoriety? Developing a life-saving vaccine? The list of possible accomplishments is endless. One could certainly include raising the dead in the class of extraordinary feats. **[Luke 7:11-15]** And yet, is raising the dead, or any other miracle for that matter, in and of itself success? No.

In order to stay faithful to a biblical approach, one must return to the life and teachings of Jesus. The Lord charged the Jews with valuing the praise of men over and above the praise of God. **[John 5:44]** Since God is the Creator of everything, His values transcend all others. Consequently, success is determined by what the Lord deems important and worthwhile. The Father audibly praised Jesus on two occasions; during the Lord's baptism and on The Mount of Transfiguration. **[Luke 3:22, 9:35]** A closer look at the motivation and context behind each affirmation enables one to more fully appreciate these events.

The Father was lovesick for His lost children. **[John 3:16]** If He did not intervene, humanity would be lost forever to the power of sin. Jesus, being the very essence of Love, denied Himself and took on human form, thereby submitting to the heart and desires of the Father, as well as identifying with His enslaved brothers and sisters. **[Philippians 2:6-11, Hebrews 2:14-18]** Love is not proud, nor self-seeking, but rather, always protects, trusts, hopes and perseveres. Love never fails. **[1 Corinthians 13:4-5, 7-8]**

Jesus was without sin, and yet, He chose baptism. Although water baptism involves repentance, or turning away from sinful living, the practice also encompasses the renunciation of worldly values and identities. Jesus the son of Mary and Joseph ceased to exist as He went under the water, and Jesus the Son of God came up empowered by the Holy Spirit. And the Father praised Him.

Jesus discussed His death, resurrection and the personal cost of following Him with His disciples immediately preceding the Father's praise on The Mount of Transfiguration. **[Luke 9:21-27]** The Lord told His disciples to take up their crosses daily. **[Luke 9:23]** He made it very clear, *"For whoever wants to save his life will lose it, but whoever loses his life for me will save it."* **[Luke 9:24]** Is this why the Father admonished Peter, James and John to listen to Jesus? **[Luke 9:35]** Is self-sacrifice the key to true success?

According to scripture, then, in order to gain the affirmation of the Father like the Lord Jesus Christ one must passionately pursue God's interests. **[John 5:30]** In so doing, the believer utterly rejects the values and standards of this world. The kingdom of God completely clashes with earthly empires. Light and darkness cannot coexist. Jesus instructed believers to seek first the kingdom of God. **[Luke 12:31]** His instruction continued:

Do not be afraid, little flock, for your Father has been pleased to give you the kingdom. Sell your possessions and give to the poor. Provide purses for yourselves that will not wear out, a treasure in heaven that will not be exhausted, where no thief comes near and no moth destroys. For where treasure is, there your heart will be also. **[Luke 12:32-34]**

God's view of success and that of Institutional Christianity's are entirely opposed to one another.

OVERCOMING

How does a true believer succeed? Scripture says, *"Who is it that overcomes the world? Only he who believes that Jesus is the Son of God."* [**1 John 5:5**] Overcoming is simply another way of describing victory. So, like everything else the believer does, he or she follows Jesus' example. Why? Because Jesus is Lord and He alone defines success.

Scripture says:

This is the one who came by water and blood--Jesus Christ. He did not come by water only, but by water and blood. And it is the Spirit who testifies because the Spirit is the truth. For there are three that testify: the Spirit, the water and the blood; and the three are in agreement. We accept man's testimony, but God's testimony is greater because it is the testimony of God, which he has given about his Son. [**1 John 5:6-9**]

Jesus fully embraced His identity as the Son of God through water baptism, and in turn, He fully rejected the ways of the world. Only after shedding His pure, untainted blood on behalf of sinful creation was the Lord's earthly mission completed. Although Jesus was and is fully God, He nevertheless took on human form and thereby accepted human limitations. The God/Man could never redeem humankind from the rule and reign of Satan or the power of sin without the empowerment of the Holy Spirit. Thus, the three are in agreement and testify: the Spirit, the water and the blood.

At the moment an individual embraces Jesus as Lord and Savior, he or she is instantaneously and entirely cleansed from past, present and future sins by the blood. Jesus' personhood and sacrifice are forever bound together. His cleansing blood is appropriated to all of one's life. The Spirit empowers believers to witness like Jesus. Eventually, each disciple becomes a living testimony. The true believer becomes lovesick and chooses the Lover's interests over and above his or her own, even to the point of death. Does this mean martyrdom? For some it does. Others, however, are compelled to pick up their crosses and die daily. *"They overcame him (the devil) by the blood of the Lamb and the word of their testimony; they did not love their lives so much as to shrink from death."* **[Revelation 12:11]**

Sadly, most are unable to shake the allure of success, or its evil parent's money and power and embrace the cost of discipleship. **[Matthew 19:16-26]** Success can and does seduce even the most faithful. Each and every person possesses an innate need for significance. Real significance is found exclusively in Jesus Christ, and consequently, lived through an overcoming lifestyle. However, as demonstrated, God's view of success completely contradicts Institutional Christianity's. Only in accordance with Jesus' life and teachings is true success experienced.

In the age of technology, success' force and power overwhelms most folks, believers and unbelievers alike. It permeates every aspect of culture and society: family, school, sports, business, government, media and entertainment. No one overcomes the seductive force of success without the inner workings of the Holy Spirit. Overcoming also necessitates great courage. Will believers, like Jesus, seek the praise of God or the praise of men? Perhaps this is why so few overcome. An absence of fortitude keeps most Christians enslaved.

John the apostle provided believers with a powerful promise, but also a dire warning:

He who overcomes will inherit all this, and I will be his God and he will be my son. But the cowardly, the unbelieving, the vile, the murderers, the sexually immoral, those who practice magic arts, the idolaters and all liars--their place will be in the fiery lake of burning sulfur. **[Revelation 21:7-8]**

CONCLUDING COMMENTS

In this chapter, and the previous two, I discussed the idolatrous notions of money, power and success. Ideological underpinnings were severed. Each sacred cow was exposed and shown for what it truly represents, a satanic delusion. Money is Mammon. Power is control. Success is fan-fare. Every Sunday, idolatrous Christians worship at least one if not all of these revered beasts. Institutional Christianity couldn't forsake temporal pleasures and eventually married the world.

However, God won the clash of kingdoms; Love conquered sin. Although Satan is defeated, he continues to exact as much carnage as possible. His effective, albeit losing strategy relies on seductive deception. He duped Adam and Eve. He found a willing vessel in Jezebel. Satan even tempted Jesus, but was rebuked for his efforts.

There is one way and one way only to resist the grandeur of money, power, and success, or for that matter any satanic device. Love the Lord thy God with all your heart. When a believer stands in the glory of God the Father through the cleansing work of the Lord Jesus Christ earthly riches pale and become inconsequential. The love of God is the secret place of the Most High. It offers divine peace and rest.

Nothing, absolutely nothing, can snatch the overcoming believer from the love of God. **[John 10:27-30]**

Spiritual Warfare and Prayer

"God speaks in the silence of the heart. Listening is the beginning of prayer."

MOTHER TERESA

I was once a strong advocate of spiritual warfare. I fought as a prayer warrior. I did my senior seminar on prayer while in seminary. I read every book on prayer and spiritual warfare that I could get my hands on. I organized all night prayer meetings. I faithfully attended early morning intercession. I belonged to a select group of intercessors. I travelled to distant countries and waged war. I visited historical sites and performed strange acts. I joined the deliverance movement. I participated in several reconciliatory events. I drove and flew to spiritual hot spots. I hosted and attended conferences. I won't presume to say I did it all, but pretty darn close. I threw my heart into each and every endeavor and I did it for years. But, once again, I was wrong.

I'm not cynical, nor disillusioned. Instead, I'm filled with immense joy. I'm more committed to prayer than I've ever been. I believe the unseen world is absolutely real. I now see ministering spirits and demonic entities with greater   frequency. I don't know if this is good or bad it just happens. So, what's the difference? I no longer listen to the so-called authorities, but to the Spirit of the living Christ. I read as much as before, and yet, every book must bear the weight of scripture.

In the following pages, I provide a brief overview of spiritual warfare. I expose misinterpreted scripture. I discuss what prayer is and isn't. I include personal experiences.

SPIRITUAL WARFARE

The underlying premise behind spiritual warfare is that powerful demonic forces rule people and often entire cultures. Unless folks are delivered from these evil entities they will continue to live under the reign of Satan and ultimately perish in everlasting darkness. Battle lines are drawn between the forces of light and the forces of darkness for the souls of humankind. Not only do evil powers affect people, but all dimensions of creation: relationships, education, politics, families, entertainment, finances, health, land, crops, weather and industry. And, as demonstrated earlier in the kingdom narrative, Satan's chief currency is sin which ultimately culminates in death. Consequently, if spiritual warriors evict rulers in high places, then the kingdom of God can be firmly established thereby allowing humanity and creation to experience abundant life. Spiritual warriors would undoubtedly characterize themselves as the Air Force in the kingdom of God; they battle in the heavenly realms.

Strategies vary depending on conditions and circumstances. Spiritual warriors' pray against spirits of lust in front of porn shops and strip clubs. Intercessors stand on mountaintops and attempt to pull down wicked principalities ruling over cities. Others perform reconciliatory acts on forgotten battlefields. A few wash the feet of disenfranchised people groups. Strategists dig into historical documents and formulate intelligence reports detailing demonic strongholds.

Clergy and churches unite in concerted fronts. And still others travel to world-renowned places to challenge principalities. I have.

Do these acts change anything? I've read about and heard stories of transformation in Central America, Argentina, Fiji, South Korea and Africa. Supposedly, entire communities from the top down or the bottom up, depending on one's perspective, are transformed. Could be. I haven't visited these places.

Nevertheless, I've yet to witness a citywide transformation here in the West. How is that? Why do these strategies work overseas, but not here? Have westerners not prayed long enough or hard enough? Does transformation require more Christians? Or, is the West ruled by the darkest and most powerful entities?

I'm not a skeptic. In fact, I'm the furthest thing from it. I probably believe too easily sometimes. I have no problem believing individuals received gold teeth, gems materialized, new hair sprouted, fat disappeared, government officials got saved, crops grew at biblical proportions, weather changed, peace enveloped a community, tribal enemies became friends and jails closed. Extra-biblical events and experiences are often real and genuine. The issue is, however, who gets the glory? A miracle worker? Or, the Lord Jesus Christ?

What does the Bible say about spiritual warfare?

MISINTERPRETED SCRIPTURE

The most misunderstood passage in the spiritual warfare movement is **Ephesians 6:11-18**:

Put on the full armor of God so that you can take your stand against the devil's schemes. For our struggle is not against flesh and blood, but against the rulers, against the authorities, against the powers of the dark world and against the spiritual forces of evil in the heavenly realms. Therefore put on the full armor of God, so that when the day of evil comes, you may be able to stand your ground, and after you have done everything, to stand. Stand firm then, with the belt of truth buckled around your waist, with the breastplate of righteousness in place, and with your feet fitted with the readiness that comes from the gospel of peace. In addition to all this, take up the shield of faith, with which you can extinguish all the flaming arrows of the evil one. Take the helmet of salvation and the sword of the Spirit, which is the word of God. And pray in the Spirit on all occasions with all kinds of prayers and requests. With this in mind, be alert and always keep on praying for all the saints.

The spiritual warfare movement is predicated upon this very text. Paul identified the real enemy as evil forces in high places. **[Vs. 12]** Believers don't battle flesh and blood, but rather, the evil forces manipulating humanity. **[Vs. 12]** He itemized the believer's spiritual armor. **[Vs. 13-17]** The weapon of choice is the sword of the Spirit. **[Vs. 17]** And lastly, believers should pray on all occasions. **[Vs. 18]**

The tone of this entire passage is spiritual in nature. From here, and other key biblical texts, spiritual warriors launch themselves into heavenly warfare. **[Matthew 16:18-19, 2 Corinthians 2:11, 10:3-5]** They construct elaborate formulas for everything from casting out demons to profiling principalities. Sometimes their strategies work and accurately portray certain circumstances. Is this because of special revelation or the goodness of God? Probably the latter.

Regardless, spiritual pragmatism cannot overrule biblical integrity. Being biblical is paramount.

If warfare enthusiasts are correct, then Paul's life and other writings should reinforce their doctrines. Scripture interprets scripture. And, even more importantly, Jesus' life and teachings must substantiate those claims too. Nowhere in Acts does Paul or any other apostle for that matter, seek, confront or challenge spiritual rulers in high places. There is not one single example. All the Pauline epistles fail on this point as well. Jesus never once sought or arrogantly challenged a principality. If anything, picking spiritual fights is satanic. **[Isaiah 14:12-15, Matthew 4:1-11, Acts 13:6-11, 16:16-18]**

Conversely, Jesus went through the countryside proclaiming the kingdom of God and freeing captives all along the way. **[Matthew 4:23]** When the Lord encountered a demonized person, He drove the demon(s) away. **[Mark 5:1-20]** The disciples followed His example. After Pentecost, and the filling of the Holy Spirit, the disciples prayed for greater boldness to speak the word of God and for more healings and miraculous signs. **[Acts 4:28-31]** They preached the kingdom of God like their Lord and Savior, Jesus.

Confused, insecure believers chase and attack dark powers. I did. The war in the heavenlies ended with Jesus' death and resurrection. *"It is finished."* **[John 19:30]** Jesus won. Every dark power, including Satan, is defeated. **[Matthew 28:18]** Confident, self-assured believers rest in the supremacy of Jesus. There's nothing more to prove.

So, what did Paul mean when he said, *"For our struggle is not against flesh and blood, but against the rulers, against the authorities, against the powers of this dark world and against the spiritual forces of evil in the heavenly realms."* **[Ephesians 6:12]** Once again, scripture interprets scripture. Paul explains himself. He goes on to say:

"Pray also for me, that whenever I open my mouth, words may be given me so that I will fearlessly make known the mystery of the gospel, for which I am an ambassador in chains. Pray that I may declare it fearlessly, as I should." **[Ephesians 6:19-20]**

Wherever the kingdom of God is preached and invades demonic strongholds, darkness gets stirred up. Evil powers refuse to relinquish their captives. In turn, these wicked entities use captives to persecute, and often times kill the children of light. Paul was lashed five times, beaten with rods three times, stoned, shipwrecked, spent a day and night in open seas, arrested, imprisoned, persecuted by Jews and gentiles and more. **[2 Corinthians 11:24-29]**

People blame people. It's human nature. Paul, like any normal human being, was undoubtedly tempted to blame his persecutors only he possessed greater revelation than most believers then and now. He knew the true cause of his troubles; evil powers controlling human puppets. To   condemn his persecutors was to overlook the real struggle occurring behind the scenes.

In Paul's time and today, Christians are persecuted. In order for believers to endure and victoriously overcome their trials and tribulations, they must utilize the spiritual armory at their disposal. Spirit defeats flesh. Otherwise, believers slide into condemnation and bitterness and like their persecutors they began to hate those who hate them. A Christian's attitude should be the same as the Lord

Jesus Christ's, *"Father, forgive them, for they do not know what they are doing."* **[Luke 23:34]** Only through the empowerment of the Holy Spirit do believers attain this attitude of heart. However, even then, with all the evil raging in the world, a Christ-like attitude is a very, very difficult thing to maintain. **[Romans 8:26-27]**

The love of God compels the children of God. Real spiritual warriors darken the doors of gentleman's clubs and invite strippers to their fellowships. True intercessors befriend gang members and hang out with disenfranchised peoples. True disciples commune with the Father rather than tallying the evils of a community. Clergy and churches unite because they deeply love each other. Instead of traveling to Timbuktu, genuine believers share their faith with neighbors. That's spiritual warfare. As believers move in love and free the captives, they will encounter the stiffest opposition of their lives.

Another classic spiritual warfare text is **Matthew 16:18-19**: *And I tell you that you are Peter, and on this rock I will build my church, and the gates of Hades will not overcome it. I will give you the keys of the kingdom of heaven: whatever you bind on earth will be bound in heaven, and whatever you loose on earth will be loosed in heaven.*

According to spiritual warfare advocates, although Jesus spoke specifically to Peter and the other disciples, His promise applied to every believer. It does. Jesus is the chief Cornerstone on which all else stands. Peter and the first disciples were foundational to the establishment of the church. Yet, because each believer is a son or daughter of the Most High they too enjoy kingdom privileges and authority. **[Romans 8:1-17]**

Because the Lord Jesus Christ entrusted the church with the keys of the kingdom of heaven believers possess power and authority over dark forces, or the gates of Hades. Therefore, once again, according to the warfare advocates believers can bind wicked powers on earth and in heaven. They are also able to loose humanity from the bondages of sin, such as poverty or addictions.

Does the warfare doctrine of 'binding and loosing' accurately portray Jesus' life and teachings? As this book has demonstrated throughout, the Lord Jesus Christ is tantamount to understanding scripture. He is Light and upon Him all the mysteries of the kingdom of God hang. **[John 1:4-5]**

First of all, what are the keys of the kingdom of heaven? Keys lock and unlock. Keys imply ownership and authority, and consequently, trust. For example, not everyone has a key to my apartment. I've only trusted family with spare keys.

Jesus did the same. He entrusted the keys to the kingdom of heaven with His spiritual family. However, take notice; scripture says keys and not key. **[Vs. 19]** How many keys are there? And what does each key represent?

There are three keys to the kingdom. The first key is the Master Key, or the Lord Jesus Christ. No one enters the kingdom of God except through Jesus. **[John 10:9, 14:6, Revelation 3:7]** An ongoing, intimate relationship with the Lord Jesus Christ is required for those desiring kingdom citizenship.

The other two keys are derived from the Master. **John 1:14** says, *"The Word became flesh and made his dwelling among us. We have* *seen his glory, the glory of the One and Only who came from the Father, full of grace and truth."*

Grace and truth represent the other two keys. Grace is love. Truth constitutes reality; it doesn't change. Scripture is truth. Each key, grace and truth, determines the affairs of earth and stretches into heaven and throughout eternity.

Truth binds. Most folks have heard the phrase, 'The truth is binding.' When a person is confronted with truth, he or she becomes accountable. Newfound knowledge demands responsibility. People are answerable in proportion to their knowledge and understanding of truth.

Grace loosens. Forgiveness flows from love. Divine kindness, because of its very nature, is impartially extended to all. Grace gives and expects no return.

Jesus also said, *"the gates of Hades will not overcome it."* **[Vs. 18]** In this verse, 'it' designates the church. However, what are the gates of Hades?

The gates of Hades signify the entry and exit point to the kingdom of darkness. Gates are defensive rather than offensive. These barriers hold those inside captive (lost humanity) while preventing rescuers (believers) from freeing. The kingdom of darkness is an evil bastion of hell surrounded by the kingdom of God, and not vice versa. Light overwhelms darkness.

The first gate of hell is lies. Satan is a liar and the father of lies. **[John 8:44]** From the very beginning, he led humanity astray through deception. **[Genesis 3:1-5]**

The second gate represents fear. After Adam and Eve sinned, they were full of fear and hid from God. **[Genesis 3:8-10]** It paralyzes and prevents those seeking asylum from leaving the confines of their spiritual bondage. Freedom is costly, but, when fear bars the way liberty seems all the more unattainable.

Spiritual warriors stand outside the gates of Hades and rail against the dark, evil powers inside. Similar to the prophets of Baal, these ignorant believers jump up and down, shouting and screaming and waving their fists in an effort to defeat demonic entities. **[1 Kings 18:26-29]** Some go so far as to taunt and belittle and eventually pay a horrible price. **[Jude 8-10]** Their spiritual antics prove ineffectual, and ultimately, do more harm than good.

Spiritual warriors forget that the kingdom of darkness was totally defeated at the cross. **[Colossians 2:15]** Jesus rules over every satanic being. The keys to the kingdom of heaven represent divine authority. When believers exercise godly authority, they use the keys given to them by Jesus.

Scripture explains scripture. Believers are to take the keys to the kingdom of heaven and unlock the gates of Hades. The key of truth opens the gate of lies. Jesus said, *"Then you will know the truth, and the truth will set you free."* **[John 8:32]** Likewise, the key of grace, or love, unlocks fear. John the apostle said, *"There is no fear in love. But perfect love drives out fear, because fear has to do with punishment. The one who fears is not made perfect in love."* **[1 John 4:18]** Once the captives step through the gates of Hades, they immediately enter the kingdom of heaven through the Lord Jesus Christ. Truth plus grace equals Life, or Jesus. If more believers used their keys hell would experience a mass exodus.

This interpretation clarifies other misused verses as well. Jesus refers to **Matthew 16:19** in **Matthew 18:18**:

I tell you the truth, whatever you bind on earth will be bound in heaven, and whatever you loose on earth will be loosed in heaven.

This verse is sandwiched between teachings on church discipline and forgiveness, and makes no reference to heavenly battles. Jesus described the steps to disciplining a wayward believer in **Matthew 18:15-17**; the offender is confronted individually, and eventually by the entire church. If the wayward believer refuses to repent through progressive, gentle correction, he or she is to be treated as a pagan or a tax collector. And how did Jesus treat pagans and tax collectors? He demonstrated special grace by fellowshipping with them. **[Matthew 11:19]**

How are sinful believers confronted? With the key of truth. Truth exposes error or lies. Believers and unbelievers alike are bound by truth. It doesn't change. Folks must alter their lifestyles in order to accommodate truth (scripture), rather than truth (scripture) accommodating believers. Truth also reveals the dangers and pitfalls of the world. Yet, if this person continues in error, he or she reenters the kingdom of darkness and comes under the domain of Satan. Is this what Paul meant when he told the Corinthians to turn an immoral brother over to Satan? **[1 Corinthians 5:4-5]** I think so.

God allows obstinate believers to have whatever they want. Believers quickly forget the sorrows experienced while living in the world. Love does not exist behind the gates of Hades. The kingdom of darkness is completely devoid of kindness. Hence, enticing, sinful pleasures mature almost overnight into death and destruction.

However, there's always hope with the Lord Jesus Christ. Jesus went on to say:

Again, I tell you that if two of you on earth agree about anything you ask for, it will be done for you by my Father in heaven. For where two or three come together in my name, there I am with them. **[Matthew 18:19-20]**

The faithful intercede on behalf of wayward believers. God is Love and His followers love sinful brothers and sisters, and even enemies. **[Luke 6:27-28]** Believers pray for those who've lost their way. God responds to intercession by drawing prodigals home and restoring them. **[Luke 15]**

Peter asked Jesus how many times he should forgive his brother. **[Matthew 18:21]** Jesus replied, *"seventy-seven times."* **[Matthew 18:22]** Or, in other words, always. God forgives. The Lord then told the parable of The Unmerciful Servant. **[Matthew 18:23-35]** In the parable, a king demonstrated great mercy by canceling a servant's large debt. **[Vs. 23-27]** However, this very same servant refused to overlook a small debt incurred by another. The king was made aware of the double standard, became infuriated and threw the unmerciful servant in prison to be tortured until he repaid his debt. **[Vs. 28-34]** Jesus finished the parable by saying, *"This is how my heavenly Father will treat each of you unless you forgive your brother from your heart."* **[Vs. 35]**

Believers loose offenders from transgressions by extending the key of grace. Mercy flows through grace. The Lord grants forgiveness to all who would receive His mercy and believers are obligated to do the same; *"Freely you have received, freely give."* **[Matthew 10:8]** Forgiveness unchains captives from the trappings of guilt, and consequently, fear.

Paul reinforced Jesus' teachings. He told the Corinthians to forgive and comfort a wayward believer who had apparently repented, *"Now instead, you ought to forgive and comfort him, so that he will not be overwhelmed by excessive sorrow. I urge you, therefore, to reaffirm your love for him".* **[2 Corinthians 2:7-8]**

Is this the immoral brother spoken of in **1 Corinthians 5**? Might be.

Jesus said: *"If you forgive anyone his sins, they are forgiven; if you do not forgive them they are not forgiven."* **[John 20:23]** As ambassadors of Christ, believers continue the Lord's ministry of forgiveness. **[2 Corinthians 5:20]** When people reject the Gospel, there remains no other means of reconciliation. Earthly decisions bind or loose and echo throughout heaven, and once again, throughout eternity.

Jesus told His disciples, *"If anyone will not welcome you or listen to your words, shake the dust off your feet when you leave that home or town. I tell you the truth, it will be more bearable for Sodom and Gomorrah on the day of judgment than for that town."* **[Matthew 10:14-15]** The disciples preached the kingdom of God. **[Matthew 10:7]** There is no kingdom without a king, or the Lord Jesus Christ. Once again, if people reject Jesus, or Truth, then they choose darkness over Light and hope begins to fade. Only through the person of the Lord Jesus Christ can people experience freedom from the bondages of sin and the dominion of Satan. And, as Jesus states in this passage earthly choices carry eternal ramifications.

Spiritual warfare advocates apply their erroneous interpretation of binding and loosing to **2 Corinthians 10:3-6**:

For though we live in the world, we do not wage war as the world does. The weapons we fight with are not weapons of the world. On the contrary, they have divine power to demolish strongholds. We demolish arguments and every pretension that sets itself up against the knowledge of God, and we take captive every thought to make it obedient to Christ. And we will be ready to punish every act of disobedience, once your obedience is complete.

Supposedly, spiritual warriors can bind or take authority over ungodly thoughts. In turn, God enforcers loose the Holy Spirit and angels against pretentious mindsets and situations, or strongholds.

First of all, individuals are going to think what they want to think. Thoughts arise from the issues of the heart.   Everyone has convictions. Even God won't control or manipulate the human spirit. Nevertheless, believers can and do war against ungodly thoughts and convictions.

What are the believer's spiritual weapons? Paul referred to weapons (plural) and not weapon. He provided a clue in **2 Corinthians 6:7**, *"...with weapons of righteousness in the right hand and in the left..."* Paul fought with multiple weapons, and so should every believer.

What is righteousness? Some say righteousness is godly conduct or living according to biblical principles. This view would include the law. Others maintain that righteousness is synonymous with justice.

Many believe righteousness constitutes the character and values of God.

Jesus said, *"But seek first his kingdom and his righteousness, and all these things will be given to you as well."* **[Matthew 6:33]** Righteousness tops the list of God's priorities. The Lord also said, *"Blessed are those who hunger and thirst for righteousness, for they will be filled."* **[Matthew 5:6]** Righteousness satisfies and quenches spiritual longing.

Jesus engaged a Samaritan woman drawing water from a well. **[John 4:1-26]** He told her, *"...Everyone who drinks this water will be thirsty again, but whoever drinks the water I give him will never thirst. Indeed, the water I give him will become in him a spring of water welling up to eternal life."* **[Vs. 13-14]** He later declares Himself to be the Messiah. **[Vs. 26]** Apparently, then, the Lord Jesus Christ is the One who satisfies the hunger and thirst of those seeking righteousness. Jesus is the Righteousness of God. **[1 John 2:1]** So, when Jesus said to seek first his kingdom and his righteousness He was referring to Himself. Once again, there is no kingdom without a king.

Other scriptures similarly bear witness. The Lord Jesus Christ stated, *"...No servant is greater than his master. If they persecuted me, they will persecute you also. If they obeyed my teaching, they will obey yours also. They will treat you this way because of my name..."* **[John 15:20-21]** With these two verses in mind, another beatitude gets fleshed out, *"Blessed are those who are persecuted because of righteousness, for theirs is the kingdom of heaven."* **[Matthew 5:10]** Believers are persecuted because of the name of Jesus or Righteousness. In order to belong to the kingdom of heaven one must enter through Jesus and Him alone.

Paul spoke of the sword of the spirit, or the word of God, in **Ephesians 6:17**. Here, word is derived from the Greek term rhema, meaning a matter or situation. **[Biblos Ephesians 6:17]** And so, when a need arises the Spirit of God provides a fresh word of insight into a particular matter. The revelatory giftings of the Holy Spirit fills one hand of the believer.

Hebrews 4:12-13 says:

For the word of God is living and active. Sharper than any double-edged sword, it penetrates even to dividing soul and spirit, joints and marrow; it judges the thoughts and attitudes of the heart. Nothing in all of creation is hidden from God's sight. Everything is uncovered and laid bare before the eyes of him to whom we must give account.

In this context, however, word means logos signifying written statement or scripture. **[Biblos Hebrews 4:12]** Scripture, then, exposes a person's thoughts and attitudes. Paul supported this point in **2 Timothy 3:16-17**:

All scripture is God breathed and is useful for teaching, rebuking, correcting, and training in righteousness, so that the man of God may be thoroughly equipped for every good work.

Scripture is the second weapon of righteousness. The believer holds the word of God in his other hand. If a person's thoughts and attitudes, whether believer or unbeliever, don't align with scripture, he or she is wrong-headed and in error. The word of God is truth. **[John 17:17]** Jesus is the Word of God or Truth. **[John 1:1-2]** The testimony of Jesus is the spirit of prophecy. **[Revelation 19:10]** The

Lord is the standard for all of existence. When a believer entertains pretentious thoughts that contradict the life and teachings of Jesus, he or she is unknowingly constructing an evil mindset or stronghold. Consequently, revelatory giftings and scripture demolish evil mindsets and take captive every thought which attempts to exalt itself above the knowledge of God.

2 Corinthians 3:7-9 says:

Now if the ministry that brought death, which was engraved in letters on stone, came with glory, so that the Israelites could not look steadily at the face of Moses because of its glory, fading though it was, will not the ministry of the Spirit be even more glorious? If the ministry that condemns men is glorious, how much more glorious is the ministry that brings righteousness!

The ministry of the Holy Spirit ushers in righteousness, or the Lord Jesus Christ, and represents the believer's primary weapon. Remember, the Spirit wields the word of God as situations arise. **[Ephesians 6:17]** Without the Spirit of truth scripture is meaningless or at best, confusing; it butchers instead of fostering life. However, those who have the Spirit of God are led into all truth. **[John 16:13]**

I've found myself extremely frustrated over the last few months. Folks with smug, know-it-all attitudes keep trying to school me. They bend their ears to official rhetoric and then quote so-called authorities. Professionals, whether in the field of medicine, law enforcement, government, entertainment, sports, media, education, business, or even religion are mere titleholders. Status, accomplishments and letters behind a name weigh heavily with the world, but are virtually worthless before God. Conversely, God evaluates all of creation   according to His Son, while the world chooses to ignore the Lord Jesus Christ. **[John 1:10-13]** Only those who possess the Spirit of Christ can discern between soul and spirit, heaven and earth, and of course truth and error.

Most people, including Christians, immerse themselves in the world, and as a result, their identity and citizenship are found here as well. Because these people love this world, they look to temporal titleholders for personal validation.

I once knew a woman who fancied herself as a prophetess. She lived on the words of others, and quite often, reiterated their prophecies. Instead of going to the throne of grace and obtaining a fresh word, she'd power up her computer, surf the Internet and parrot conference prophets.

I know another person who packs around periodicals. He ties the information together, and like a conspiracy theorist, formulates possible outcomes. He fails to grasp the distinction between information and revelation.

Each person hopes to gain special insight by resorting to worldly methodologies. Genuine revelation comes from the heart of God. The Spirit of truth illuminates the mysteries found in Jesus.

Paul reinforced Jesus' teaching when he said:

The Spirit searches all things, even the deep things of God. For who among men knows the thoughts of a man except the man's spirit within him? In the same way no one knows the thoughts of God except the Spirit of God. We have not received the spirit of the world but the Spirit who is from God that we may understand what God has freely given us. This is what we speak, not in words taught us by human wisdom but in words taught by the Spirit, expressing spiritual truths in spiritual words. The man without the Spirit does not accept the things that come from the Spirit of God, for they are foolishness to him, and he cannot understand them, because they are spiritually discerned. The spiritual man makes judgments about all things, but he himself is not subject to any man's judgment... **[1 Corinthians 2:10-15]**

John concurred:

You, dear children, are from God and have overcome them (antichrists), because the one who is in you is greater than the one who is in the world. They are from the world and therefore speak from the viewpoint of the world, and the world listens to them. We are from God, and whoever knows God listens to us; but whoever is not from God does not listen to us. This is how we recognize the Spirit of truth and the spirit of falsehood. **[1 John 4:4-6]**

The greatest weapon any believer possesses is the presence of God in the form of the Holy Spirit. The Spirit separates truth from worldly arguments and viewpoints. Kingdom realities are completely foreign and strange to citizens of this world as well as earthly-minded Christians. Unless the Spirit of Christ reveals truth it remains hidden to a dark and perishing world.

In summary, the spiritual warfare movement has been predicated upon **Ephesians 6:11-18**. Elaborate formulas are constructed for everything from casting out demons to profiling principalities, and often times, with limited success. Nevertheless, spiritual pragmatism cannot overrule biblical integrity. Nowhere in scripture does Jesus, or Paul for that matter, seek and arrogantly challenge spiritual powers. Picking spiritual fights constitutes a satanic enterprise.

Jesus proclaimed the kingdom of God and freed captives. When the Lord encountered a demonized person He drove the demon(s) away. The disciples followed His example. The war in the heavenlies ended with Jesus' death and resurrection. Every dark power, including Satan, was defeated.

Wherever the kingdom of God is preached, and invades demonic strongholds, darkness gets stirred up. Wicked entities use captives to persecute and kill the children of light. People blame people. However, Paul knew the real cause of worldly troubles; evil powers controlling human puppets. In order for believers to endure persecution and overcome trials and tribulations, they must utilize the spiritual armory at their disposal. Otherwise, the children of light slide into condemnation and bitterness, and like their persecutors, they begin to hate those who hate them. A believer's attitude should be the same as the Lord Jesus Christ's, *"Father, forgive them, for they do not know what they are doing."* As the faithful move in love and free captives, they will encounter the stiffest opposition of their lives.

Another classic spiritual warfare text is **Matthew 16:18-19**. The doctrine of 'binding and loosing' evolved from this passage. Supposedly, spiritual warriors can bind evil spirits and loose captives from the bondages of sin.

Jesus entrusted the keys of the kingdom of heaven to His spiritual family. There are three keys. Jesus is the Master Key. No one enters the kingdom of heaven except through the Lord Jesus Christ. Grace and truth represent the other two keys. Grace is love and loosens. Truth binds.

The gates of Hades stand for the entry and exit point for the kingdom of darkness. These barriers hold those inside captive (lost humanity) while preventing rescuers (believers) from freeing. The first gate is lies and the second fear. Spiritual warriors stand outside the gates and rail against evil powers inside the fortress of hell. The key of truth unlocks lies and grace opens fear. Truth plus grace equals Life, or Jesus. If believers used their keys hell would experience a mass exodus.

This interpretation clarifies **Matthew 18:18** too. This verse is sandwiched between teachings on church discipline and forgiveness. Wayward believers are confronted with the key of truth. The faithful intercede on behalf of their confused brothers and sisters. Believers loose offenders from transgressions by extending the key of grace or forgiveness. Forgiveness unchains captives from the trappings of guilt, and consequently, fear. Earthly decisions bind or loose and echo throughout heaven. No hope exists outside of Jesus.

Another misconstrued text is **2 Corinthians 10:3-6**. According to those involved in the spiritual warfare movement, they can bind ungodly thoughts and loose angels and the Holy Spirit against pretentious mindsets.

Paul fought with multiple weapons of righteousness and so should every believer. Righteousness tops the list of God's priorities. It satisfies spiritual longings. Jesus is Righteousness.

Fresh revelation represents one weapon of righteousness and scripture the second. The Spirit provides rhema words and wields the logos or scripture. The spirit of prophecy is the testimony of the Lord Jesus Christ. Jesus is the Word of God. The word demolishes evil mindsets and takes captive every thought which attempts to exalt itself above the knowledge of God. The ministry of the Holy Spirit ushers in Righteousness, or the Lord Jesus Christ, and constitutes the believer's primary weapon.

Most folks, believers included, immerse themselves in the world, and as a result, their identity and citizenship are found here as well. Because these folks love this world they look to temporal titleholders for personal validation.

PRAYER

A pattern found throughout scripture, whether in the Old Testament or the New, is that God and all things associated with Him are simple. Simplicity reflects Love. Love is elemental and builds life. Conversely, complexity is the stamp of Satan and represents one of the surest signs of evil. It exalts meaningless rules while ignoring spirit. The only requirement God placed upon Adam and Eve in the Garden of Eden was to not eat from the tree of knowledge of good and evil. **[Genesis 2:17]** Everything else was acceptable.

The Lord Jesus Christ admonished His disciples to love God with all their heart, soul, mind and strength. The second greatest commandment was like the first; love your neighbor as yourself. **[Mark 12:28-34]** When one truly embraces these two commandments all others become minor, and really, insignificant.

As gentile believers were grafted into the body of Christ, church leadership made only four stipulations: abstain from food offered to idols, from sexual immorality, from the meat of strangled animals and from blood. **[Acts 15:20]**

Detractors will undoubtedly draw reference to the law. Wasn't the law detailed and complex? Yes it was. However, God instituted the law to protect His beloved children from the dangers and pitfalls of sin. Because sin is complex, and consequently evil, measures to soften or even counteract its power proved complicated until the coming of the Christ.

Other detractors cite Paul's letters to the Corinthians, or Colossians or perhaps **1st** and **2nd Timothy** as examples. Each letter provides detailed guidelines for church life. Even so, Paul's letters were written to address specific situations. As love decreases complexity increases. The alternative is also true; as love increases, complexity decreases. To the degree believers disregarded love was to the degree rules were set in place. If believers then and now took Jesus commandments to heart, especially love your neighbor as yourself, church life would become amazingly simple and freeing. This is why Paul said, *"everything is permissible-- but not everything is beneficial. Everything is permissible-- but not everything is constructive. Nobody should seek his own good, but the good of others."* **[1 Corinthians 10:23-24]**

Because God is Love, He infused all of creation with simplicity. For example, the more ingredients listed on a can of food the unhealthier the contents are for human consumption. In turn, food in its most basic form perishes quickly, such as raw vegetables and fresh fruit, but these also represent the greatest nutritional value for human consumption.

People groups with the longest life expectancies live simple lives. There are no gyms. Pharmacies aren't found on every other street corner. These individuals don't consume a cabinet full of supplements. Instead, the healthiest people seemingly walk everywhere and garden. When gardening isn't an option, like in city centers, these folks purchase fresh produce at local markets. They drink water and sip red wine with family and friends. Meaningful relationships are vital to personal welfare.

Avid climbers scale rock faces without ropes. Serious fishermen design their own tackle. Hardcore swimmers free-dive. Master chefs use fresh ingredients. Pushups and pull-ups work better than exercise machines. Less is more. Simple.

Prayer is simple, too. And yet... confused believers create long, elaborate formulas for communicating with God. If one prays like 'this,' then God responds like 'that.' They define what intercession is and isn't. Thanksgiving must be offered at precise moments. Books are penned by professional pray-ers and reveal correct protocol and format. According to some, God even requires a journal. Early morning prayer groups storm the throne of grace, or lay hold of the horns of the alter, and demand that their requests be answered. Warriors scream and shout at heavenly beings. 24/7 houses of prayer have sprung up the world over.

I recently underwent a heart-wrenching experience. While walking along the river with the Lord, He said to me, "Walter, I don't have very many good friends." My eyes welled up, and I began to cry. But, worst of all, my heart broke. Even now tears form. My Father, the Lord of the universe, the God of all creation, the kindest and most loving Being one could ever imagine, lacked good friends. I felt horrible.

The masses of so-called Christians are like spoiled, self-centered kids who only want and take from God. They want Him to fix their rebellious children. They demand new things. They bash enemies. They judge neighbors. Their intercession amounts to nothing more than whining. They tell God what He owes them. They expect blessings. They pray for worldly success. Ultimately, petty Christians use prayer as a means of fulfilling personal ambitions. Arrogance fuels the prevailing attitude of entitlement.

Interestingly enough, the Father, in His immeasurable goodness, regularly and graciously answers prayers regardless of motivation. He loves even the most selfish people, and consequently, blesses each and every person.

I've witnessed this pettiness in the world too. One couple in particular comes to mind. They're wealthy by most human standards. Sadly, however, their children and a few fair-weathered friends only show up when they want something-- money. And, like the gracious God they serve, this couple generously gives.

Prayer is intimacy with God and Him alone. If believers remember this one all-important truth, their relationship with the Lord will mature and grow throughout eternity.

God no longer dwells in a temple built by hands, but in the human spirit. **[Acts 17:24]** Any believer who calls on the name of the Lord Jesus Christ is the living, breathing temple of God. **[1 Corin-**

thians 3:16-17] Christ lives in the Father, and believers live in Him. **[John 14:20]**

When Jesus drove the money changers from the temple of God, He declared, "*...My house will be called a house of prayer...*" **[Matthew 21:13]** Jesus' action and statement were prophetic. Once again, believers represent the temple of God. Therefore, those things that detract from prayer, or intimacy with Lord must be driven out. The Spirit of the living Christ dispels religious positioning, greed and worldly pursuits from the hearts of believers. God refuses to reside with evil ambitions.

Jesus gave His very Spirit to dwell in believers forever and as a deposit of things to come. **[John 14:16-17, 2 Corinthians 1:22]** As a man and a woman are joined in marriage and the two become one flesh, so too does a believer unite with the Holy Ghost, spirit to Spirit. **[Genesis 2:24]** The believer retains her individual identity, and yet, she bonds with the Spirit of God. The Spirit empowers believers to glorify and honor the Lord Jesus Christ through word and deed. Love distinguishes true believers from false disciples. **[John 3:10]** Since God's Spirit lives in the hearts and minds of believers the Lord is always present with His beloved family. As a result, believers are able to fellowship with the Lord at anytime and anyplace; in the morning, or late at night, in the shower, or at Costco.

I can always tell who and what a person values. Individuals invest time and energy into those people and things they love. How many believers just spend time hanging out with God and give Him their full attention? Good question, isn't it? They sit through Sunday morning services. They wine and dine their wives. They coach little-league. But, do they love my Father? Do they pray? Are they His friends?

I know five of six people who continually run their mouths. They seemingly know everything. Whenever they have an audience of any kind these chatterboxes talk for hours on end about their favorite subject matter-- themselves. Originally, I wrote the whole annoying experience off as insecurity. It is. These motor mouths attempt to bolster their low self-esteem through hype and embellishment. But, that's only half the equation. Controlling verbosity demonstrates extreme arrogance by completely disregarding the views and convictions of others. These people are insinuating in a round-about way, 'I don't care what you think.' It is bad behavior and utterly disrespectful.

Christians treat God the same way. Instead of quieting their spirits and allowing the Lord to share His heart, believers open the floodgates and pray away. These pray-ers supposedly know what's best for themselves and everybody else. Their disrespectful behavior epitomizes presumption by ignoring the thoughts and feelings of the Father.

I'm all for praying in tongues. **[1 Corinthians 14:18]** Make requests and intercede for family, friends and everyone else, regularly. **[1 Timothy 2:1-2]** But, first show some decency, and allow the Lord to speak. Believers should spend just as much time, if not more so, listening. In so doing, their prayers will come into agreement with the heart of God. [Matthew 6:10] The Lord gains friends too. Is there any greater achievement in life than to be counted as a friend of God? I don't think so.

As believers spend time with God they grow-up. His interests become their interests. Pettiness disappears. Whining stops. Demands cease. Believers are transformed into divine royalty or legitimate sons and daughters. The children of God love the Father for who He is and not because of what they can get out of Him.

Eventually, for those who choose to abide in the Spirit, and pray without ceasing, their relationship with the Lord deepens and knows no bounds. He confides in those closest to Him. Secrets are shared between God and His best friends. The Lover trusts the beloved, and therefore, no subject matter is off limits. This intense, dynamic reality is not the goal or even the end result. It is simply pure, undefiled intimacy with the Lord.

There are no secret formulas concerning prayer. For those who claim special knowledge they're lying. Prescriptive, end-all techniques to a wonderful prayer life belong to pop-Christianity. Pull those books from the library and toss the silliness out the back door. Love cannot be contained or regulated. Only the most arrogant individuals attempt to manipulate and control intimacy. If a believer feels he or she is straying, or perhaps becoming weird, consult scripture; it's the only prayer manual written by God. Any meaningful relationship requires hard, unadulterated work... even with God. The problem is never with God, but with believers. Believers need a change of heart, not God. He's the essence of Love and they're not. But, when a person makes a lifelong commitment to God and invests their heart and soul into the relationship, he or she experiences the most exhilarating love affair ever imagined.

PERSONAL EXPERIENCE

God gave me another dream, and it wonderfully depicted my relationship with Him.

DREAM:

I found myself standing beside a crystal clear river. As I bent over and looked into the rushing water, I saw unique patterns of red rubies embedded in the river floor.

In the next frame, I was underwater, and strangely enough, able to breathe. I took my right index finger and began plucking out these magnificent gems. I glanced over, and directly beneath the spot where I originally stood, I noticed even more rubies lodged in the riverbank. I dug these gems out too.

In the third and final frame, I was once again underwater, and still able to breathe. A jeweler's display case, filled with rich and spectacular settings of green emeralds sat immediately in front of me. As I stared at this beautiful display, I saw bright red rubies shining behind the case. I swam around the case to where the rubies were laying. Here, the river floor was soft and sandy, and I scooped up a handful of gems. End of dream.

INTERPRETATION:

The river represents the flow of the Spirit. Wherever the Spirit flows there is life, and of course, heavenly riches. At one point in my journey, I witnessed the riches of the Spirit, but failed to experience these things. I possessed a certain amount of insight and readily saw numerous patterns of truth found in scripture and life.

The bright, red rubies represent wisdom and the precious truths of God. **[Proverbs 3:13-18]** Red stands for sacrifice. I stood on a number of truths long before I swam in the Spirit, but only came to that realization much later. After submerging myself in the Spirit, I began to take hold of these precious truths and apply them personally. At first, even in the Spirit, I had to dig and scratch in order to acquire the true riches of God. Over the course of my life I've often paid dearly for understanding.

The jeweler's display case filled with spectacular settings of emeralds symbolized well established, life giving tenets of Christianity: Jesus died for a lost and perishing world; The blood of Christ covers all sin; The Bible is truth; God is Love; and more. Green signifies life. God's greatest treasures are always on display for any believer who would stop and reflect upon their beauty and glory. And yet, as others and I gaze intently upon these eternal wonders, many more riches come into view. These rubies are so abundant that believers can easily scoop them up. Some are contained in this book.

As I spend time with my Father and abide in the Spirit, my prayer life flourishes. He's my best Friend and I would like to think I'm one of His. I believe I am. I need to hear Him. I need to see Him. I need to feel Him. It no longer matters what I get out of my relationship with God. I just love my best Friend and want to be with Him, always.

I've often wondered what the next leg of the journey is for my family and me as I finish writing this book. I've asked the Lord. And, as always, He responded.

While walking along the river, I stopped at a bridge. It approximates the half waypoint in my walks with the Lord. I like to stand there and reflect. On this particular day, I felt a nudge to turn my attention upwards. Interestingly, two bald eagles circled above. They were so close I could even see their eyes; each bird looked directly at me. At that moment, the Lord said, "You guys are going to soar." My concerns about the future have since vanished. I may not know all the details of the journey. Nevertheless, the Lord is in it. Everything is going to be all right. Thank You, God.

SUMMARY

The spiritual warfare movement is extreme in nature and misuses a number of important biblical texts. Rather than being kingdom-minded and recognizing the truth that Jesus has defeated any and all evil powers, spiritual warriors elevate wicked beings to a position and stature they don't deserve. If believers simply emulated the life and values of the Lord Jesus Christ, they would represent the most radical element in society today.

Jesus travelled the countryside preaching the kingdom of God. Never once, at least according to scripture, did He ever sit in the synagogue with His disciples and call down wicked powers. Instead, the Lord cast out demons, healed the sick and performed a multitude of miracles. He freed captives. After the disciples were filled with the

Holy Spirit, they followed Jesus' example and continued establishing the kingdom of God.

Believers possess the keys of the kingdom of heaven; whatever they bind on earth is bound in heaven, and likewise, whatever they loose on earth is loosed in heaven. When believers preach Jesus and Him crucified, people are bound by truth. There is no other name under heaven in which men can be saved. Moreover, in Jesus, and Him alone, is there forgiveness of sins. People are loosed from wrongdoing and guilt. The keys of the kingdom of heaven, grace and truth, unlock the gates of Hades, lies and fear.

Believers also possess spiritual weapons. Revelatory giftings enable believers to recognize ulterior motives and distinguish between soul and spirit. Scripture is the sword of the Spirit and separates truth from error. Rhema and logos words destroy pretentious mindsets that exalt themselves against the knowledge of the Most High. The very presence of God, or the Holy Spirit, is the believer's greatest weapon. The Spirit of God leads believers into all truth.

Prayer became a catchphrase for any type of ministry. In reality, prayer is an intimate relationship between believer and God, simple. Complexity, in general, indicates evil. The Lord doesn't have very many good friends.

For the believer who wholeheartedly invests in their relationship with the Lord, and allows intimacy to grow and mature, he or she will undoubtedly become God's new friend.

Inner Healing and Forgiveness

"I can forgive, but I cannot forget, is only another way of saying, I will not forgive. Forgiveness ought to be like a cancelled note-- torn in two, and burned up, so that it never can be shown against one."
HENRY WARD BEECHER

Inner healing is another popular trend found throughout segments of Institutional Christianity. The underlying thought behind inner healing is this: Life is difficult, and sometimes, flat-out evil. Therefore, hearts and souls get wounded, and require mending. The goal is always the same, wholeness. However, the methods vary significantly. Various streams and ministries have developed their own curriculums: Restoring the Foundations, Cleansing Streams, Sozo, Plumbline, Theophostic Prayer, Healing Rooms, Celebrate Recovery and other twelve step programs, Group therapy, The Elijah House, Truth encounters, deliverance, Marriage and Family Counseling, Psychology, Psychiatry, and probably a number of other therapies that I'm not aware of. The very wealthy commit to in-house treatment centers.

I've been the recipient of great kindness and patience in my darkest hours. For this, I am eternally grateful. I honestly believe I would have died if a couple of kind souls had not intervened in my life.

Nevertheless, inner healing, like so much of the subject matter presented in this book became idolatrous and miserably failed. Believers aren't changing. Something is horribly wrong.

I know a number of believers who grumble about the same old hurts incurred some five, or ten, or even twenty years ago. A broken heart pushes the play button, and all of a sudden, the poison spews out. They forever rehearse mistreatment and tragedies. Their fathers did or didn't do something to them. A number experienced mean-spirited divorces. Some lost an important person(s) in their life. A few were cheated out of money or a perceived opportunity. Others got kicked out of ministry. And a whole bunch were sexually, emotionally and spiritually abused.

Before I continue, allow me to say something very important. I have no desire to minimize another person's pain. If I'd lived through some of these same horrors that others had I would be dead, or at the very least, in prison. I thank God for sparing me. However, please understand, unless one bathes his or her offenses in God's unconditional love, and allows the wrongs to dissolve, he or she will be forever stuck in those dark moments of time and never overcome their grief.

A few of these broken souls drive all day in order to sit at the feet of the anointed minister. I know of one person who journeyed into the desert, and paid five hundred dollars for an hour session with the man of God. He supposedly broke off curses that dated back generations. However, I never witnessed any transformation in my friend. Others spend a couple of hours each week in therapy. Antidepressants soften the pain. Cutting edge Christians fly to conferences, and for a measly one hundred dollars, a specialist walks them through 'daddy' issues. A few keep casting the same demons out, over and over again. Healthy believers purchase DVD sets, and practice their newfound revelation on friends and family.

These statements aren't theories, or mere generalizations, but rather, each is based on fact. I've lived through the pain and the therapy... I've been divorced a couple times. I lost a little boy and everything else in the process. I've been kicked out of ministries. And, I've been abused. As a result, I've seen a couple of Marriage and Family Counselors, three or four psychologists, and two psychiatrists. I was diagnosed as bi-polar. I've been on a half dozen antidepressants. I went through Restoring the Foundations. I've been 'cleansed.' I've been 'Sozoed.' I've allowed the 'Inner Light' to illuminate my deep, dark wounds. I've sat through AA meetings and group therapy. I've watched Elijah House DVDs. I've listened to so-called prophets. I've had demons cast out of me, many times. And, thankfully, I was too poor to enter a treatment center.

To a greater or lesser degree, everyone is dysfunctional. Like the rest of reality, it's a spectrum, and not an either/or proposition. Almost without exception, a person's dysfunction begins during childhood or before. Even the healthiest homes are less than perfect. I grew up in a wonderful family, and yet, I have my share of problems. Individuals are flawed.

Contrary to popular opinion, and the practices of Institutional Christianity, no program provides wholeness. Wholeness lies far beyond the scope therapeutic gimmicks. There is only one sure-fired recipe for abundant life; the Lord Jesus Christ and His power to forgive.

THE LORD JESUS CHRIST

Jesus is the model for every believer. As far as I can tell from scripture, the Lord never incorporated programs. He treated each and every disciple, and all others, as unique and special individuals. Programs are for farm animals; regardless of breed, size, or age, all get treated the same.

Jesus fathered His disciples. He walked beside them. He slept by them. He ate with them. He lived with the disciples for the better part of three years. During that season, the Lord addressed the heartfelt needs of His followers. Scripture records a few of those instances. **[Mark 10:35-45, John 21:15-19]** Discipleship is spiritual parenting, and more specifically, fathering.

A father is responsible for his children. Children are the living, breathing extensions of a father. A true father loves his child more than himself. Fathers protect, guide, discipline, and when the need arises, heal. Because a father is older, and has weathered life, he can and does speak into the difficulties confronting his children. There exists a deep, abiding intimacy between father and child.

Jesus fathered because He was fathered. In general, scripture reveals very little regarding the life and person of Joseph, the earthly father of Jesus. Scripture does say, however, he was a righteous man. **[Matthew 1:19-25]** Joseph instilled those same values in Jesus. Otherwise, why would the heavenly Father have entrusted His only begotten Son to Joseph and Mary? This couple obviously possessed great depth.

The story continues. Throughout the Gospels, Jesus consistently refers to God as His Father. **[Matthew 11:27, Mark 8:38, Luke**

23:34, John 8:28] Evidently, then, God fathered Jesus too. Jesus affirms this truth by saying, *"...I do nothing on my own but speak just what the Father has taught me."* **[John 8:28]** He also said, *"All things have been committed to me by my Father. No one knows the Son except the Father, and no one knows the Father except the Son and those to whom the Son chooses to reveal him."* **[Matthew 11:27]**

What the heavenly Father imparted to Jesus, He in turn gave to His disciples. Jesus said, *"...I have called you friends, for everything that I learned from my Father I have made known to you."* **[John 15:15]** When the church was born on the day of Pentecost, the disciples hit the ground running. Each devoted himself to prayer or intimacy with the Father. **[Acts 6:4]**

A true spiritual father intimately knows God. He can and does speak into the hurts and wounds of his children. A father also ushers children into an ever-maturing relationship with God. Like begets like; fathers beget fathers.

Unless a spiritual leader spends significant time with the Father, he or she has nothing to offer others, especially the brokenhearted. Their words lack substance, and most of all, life. Most believers are orphans, and get pawned off on surrogate fathers, or at the very least, professionals. It is the proverbial blind leading the blind. **[Luke 6:39]** Since so few leaders know God, they are forced to enroll believers into foster care; hence, the plethora of inner healing techniques. Most of these techniques have worldly underpinnings. Inner healing replaced fathering as the chief means of caring for needy believers.

Jesus said:

No one can come to me unless the Father who sent me draws him, and I will raise him up on the last day. It is written in the Prophets: They will all be taught by God. Everyone who listens to the Father and learns from him comes to me... I am the bread of life. Your forefathers ate the manna in the desert, yet they died. But here is the bread that comes down from heaven, which a man may eat and not die. I am the living bread that came down from heaven. If anyone eats of this bread, he will live forever... **[John 6:44-45, 48-51]**

Peter grasped this, and said to Jesus, *"You have the words of eternal life. We believe and know that you are the Holy One of God."* **[John 6:68-69]**

Another factor deserves mentioning here. Western believers have grown fat and soft. They find themselves insulated by a politically correct culture. Insensitive remarks get blown out of proportion. Unredeemed, self-centered slights at work or in school become the greatest of evils. Rights get violated and lawsuits are filed. Pettiness owns the day.

The rest of the world doesn't understand western liberties. Many cultures have experienced ethnic and tribal genocide, as well as systematic rape. Third world believers are often ostracized and relegated to abject poverty because of their faith. A few governments imprison and torture Christians. Believers are sold into slavery. Mobs terrorize Christian families. This was also the reality for the early church.

The point being: There's always someone with a darker and more horrific story. Everyone has the ability to be thankful for something. Western believers should count their many, many blessings.

THE POWER TO FORGIVE

As stated earlier, a few folks I know continually rehash old hurts. I've asked them on a number of different occasions, "Have you forgiven ___?" Their immediate response is always something like, 'Oh, I did that a long time ago.' or 'Of course I did.' At first, I believed them. Yet, every time a particular person was brought up in our conversation, their emotions flared; one or two became very angry and snarled, most wept and all recounted their ordeals with vivid detail. If these folks had really forgiven, then why all the emotional baggage? Why the ongoing hurt? A person remains in bondage as long as the offender, dead or alive, can continue to tug on the victim's heartstrings.

I've told believers to forgive according to their faith. In other words, even though a believer may not feel like forgiving, according to scripture, he or she must forgive. **[Matthew 18:23-35]** When a believer makes a conscious decision to forgive a debtor, his or her feelings eventually catch up to that decision over a period of time. Hence, the proverbial saying, 'Time heals all wounds.' And in most cases, this strategy works; an offense gradually fades, and then altogether disappears. But, most of the time is not the same as 'always.' In a number of cases, a hurt, even after many, many years refuses to fade let alone disappear altogether.

Some maintain that there is a vast difference between forgiving and forgetting; one forgives an offender, but he or she doesn't forget an offense. Or, the mind ignores the debt, but the heart is still tormented by the traumatic event. This isn't forgiveness. Whenever an offense retains its power to cause grief, the victim has yet to forgive. Forgiveness and forgetfulness are inseparable. The heart, through the power of love, forgives the offender. In turn, the mind submits to the heart, and banishes the offense to the forgotten past.

The real distinction lies between forgetting and remembering. When one forgets he or she no longer considers something significant or worthwhile. The insignificant thing drifts from consciousness. Once a person truly forgives, and therefore forgets, a wrong is stripped of power and loses its ability to hurt. Nevertheless, those who forgive can still remember their past. The only difference being, the past remains a distant, lifeless shell of it's former self. Paul undoubtedly understood this truth when he said, *"...Forgetting what is behind and straining toward what is ahead..."* **[Philippians 3:13]**

There is a secret to forgiveness that enables believers to achieve inner wholeness. Only a few believers ever realize this truth, and in so doing, overcome the wounds incurred throughout life.

After Jesus had been betrayed, deserted, beaten beyond recognition, crucified and was quickly approaching death **[Mark 14:43-15]**, He said, *"Father, forgive them, for they do not know what they are doing."* **[Luke 23:34]** How did Jesus, after all He endured, still love, and extend forgiveness to His tormentors? Many will immediately state something like, 'Well, that was Jesus. No one else can love like that.' In a sense, yes. But, in another sense, no.

Joseph, an Old Testament type of Jesus, was betrayed by all of his brothers. **[Genesis 37:12-36]** Consequently, he suffered years of slavery and wrongful imprisonment. **[Genesis 39-41]** And yet, when Joseph once again encountered his brothers, he said, *"Don't be afraid. Am I in the place of God? You intended to harm me, but God intended it for good to accomplish what is now being done, the saving of many lives. So then, don't be afraid. I will provide for you and your children."* **[Genesis 50:20-21]**

After the Israelites vehemently opposed Moses on several occasions **[Exodus 5:21, 14:12, 15:24, 16:2, 17:3]**, he went before the Lord and prayed, *"Turn from your fierce anger; relent and do not bring disaster on your people."* **[Exodus 32:12]**

Paul, who experienced the most severe form of persecution **[2 Corinthians 11:23-27]**, said, *"Here is a trustworthy saying that deserves full acceptance: Christ Jesus came into the world to save sinners-- of whom I am the worst. But for that very reason I was shown mercy so that in me, the worst of sinners, Christ Jesus might display his unlimited patience as an example for those who would believe on him and receive eternal life."* **[1 Timothy 1:15-16]** How did he do that?

As the Holy Spirit transforms believers into the image and likeness of the Lord Jesus Christ, they pass through greater and greater spheres of glory emanating from God. **[2 Corinthians 3:18]** These spheres of glory represent dimensions of love. When a believer enters a new dimension of love, it engulfs him or her and imparts new revelation. The faithful draw ever closer to the heart of the Father. Those believers who continually cultivate intimacy with the Lord, pass from immature love into deeper dimensions of sacrificial love and become more and more like Jesus who is the embodiment of Love. They can't help but forgive!

Three by-products emerge from intimacy with the Lord: The majesty of God captivates all who behold Him; Worldly aspirations lose appeal and attraction; and lastly, Believers become very aware of their own unworthiness.

The majesty of God captivates all who behold Him. His glory eclipses creation in its entirety. As believers commune with God, they become lovesick and nothing else satisfies.

Worldly aspirations lose appeal and attraction. Anything and everything pales in comparison to the presence of the Lord. Worldly pleasures seem empty and insignificant. Believers are citizens of the kingdom of heaven. Every self-centered thought and intention is exposed before God. Nothing is hidden. Consequently, no one can boast in personal righteousness. All have sinned, and fallen short of the glory of God. **[Romans 3:23]**

Joseph, Moses and Paul were all completely stripped of earthly ambitions. Each man turned and fully embraced God. Pharaoh said of Joseph, *"Can we find anyone like this man, one in whom is the spirit of God?"* **[Genesis 41:38]** The Lord spoke face to Face with Moses, as a man speaks with his friend. **[Exodus 33:11]** And Paul experienced heavenly mysteries that very few believers are ever allowed to witness. **[2 Corinthians 12:3-4]** These three great men went deep with the Lord, and became undone. Consequently, each man of God could readily forgive those who harmed him just as the Lord Jesus Christ had.

A number of believers can forgive others, but not themselves. In general, individuals who struggle in this area compare sins. These people are burdened with excessive guilt because they view their transgressions as more evil than that of others. And to be quite frank, some sins are especially wicked. Nevertheless, there exists a fatal flaw in their understanding.

Sin is sin--according to God. The Lord doesn't weigh one's transgressions against that of others in order to determine who's been naughty and who's been nice. This attitude constitutes self-righteousness, and self-righteousness is a form of pride or sin. Everyone sins and everyone is wrong. **[Romans 3:10]** From God's perspective, all people, whether one is a hardened criminal or a kind, elderly grandmother must appropriate the shed blood of the Lord Jesus Christ to be declared righteous. **[Romans 5:9-11]** Faith in Jesus and Him alone makes one righteous regardless of past, present or future sins.

A few years back, the Lord gave me a vision. I saw myself swimming downward. I strained to reach the bottom, but no matter how hard I tried I was unable to swim deep enough. Eventually, I stopped, turned upward and swam back to the surface. Upon reaching the top, I climbed out of what appeared to be a well. I looked down at myself, and quickly realized, I was drenched in blood.

The Lord revealed to me that my sins were forever lost in His blood. And no matter how hard I tried, I could never find, lay hold of, or dredge up my wrongdoings ever again. How could I not forgive myself or others?

SUMMARY

Inner healing has replaced discipleship and more specifically fathering as the chief means of addressing hurts and difficulties confronting believers today. Jesus is the model for all believers. He was fathered by Joseph, and of course, His heavenly Father. Likewise, whatever the Lord received He in turn gave to His disciples. Since so few spiritual leaders truly know God they have very little to offer others. Therefore, needy believers are pawned off on foster parents or professionals and run through inner healing programs. Most wounded believers remain stuck.

A number of believers say they've forgiven, but somehow, the past continues to haunt them. When one truly forgives another, he or she also forgets the past and banishes the event from consciousness. Real forgiveness takes the power and sting out of past offenses and these become forgotten, lifeless events.

There is a secret to forgiving others and one's self. The believer cultivates intimacy with God through the workings of the Holy Spirit. Moreover, he or she passes through greater and greater dimensions of love. Instead of dwelling in immature, self-serving love the believer experiences ever increasing dimensions of sacrificial love accompanied by newfound revelation. Ultimately, the forgiving believer is being transformed into the image and likeness of the Lord Jesus Christ.

Three by products emerge from intimacy with God: The majesty of God captivates all who behold Him; Worldly aspirations lose appeal and attraction; and lastly, Believers become very aware of their own unworthiness.

Epilogue

I've thought about this phrase time and again—"The more you know, the less you need." It's true. As I've matured over the years, albeit ever so slowly, excess, fads, hype, shiny, newer, bigger, and more of were all replaced with simplicity and function. Some people refer to this as minimalism. I don't know, could be. I've learned that empty rooms waste space. Fads quickly pass. Most people who talk a lot lie. I can only wear one pair of pants and shoes at a time. Newness lasts for a couple of weeks or a month at most. Bright lights and colors hide something. Bigness compensates for smallness. More is less. And, the majority of individuals aren't very happy.

Conversely, my little two-bedroom apartment suits my family just fine. A blue blazer is timeless. I spend more time listening than talking these days. I need one pair of running shoes for exercise and entertainment. I get as much enjoyment out of library books as current bestsellers. Some of the most extraordinary people I've ever met appear boring and even frumpy. A big chest compensates for little or no personality. Give my wife a few fresh ingredients and she can put together a meal that shames the best eateries. And, best of all, I'm happy.

Most people, and this includes believers, live externally, and consequently they rely on 'things' to foster a sense of wellbeing. Rarely, if ever, do things offer lasting fulfillment. Even the best events are short-lived. The excitement passes, and people must find something else to consume and entertain themselves with. The vicious cycle then repeats itself.

My personhood, as does everyone's, flows from knowledge. But, the question remains, knowledge of what or whom? Jesus. My intimate knowledge of Jesus changed my life. Really, for me, the bumper sticker should read, 'The more you know Jesus, the less you need.'

Almost without exception, every biblical great possessed little or nothing in terms of worldly riches and status. Each deeply loved God, and therefore, His Son the Lord Jesus Christ. Jesus owned the clothes on His back and that's all. His disciples lived the same way. The world makes no claims over those who commune with the Lord.

I spend a great deal of time talking with my best Friend. I read and reread the Gospels. Jesus interprets scripture. My wife and little boy are the joys of my life. I have a few friends who love me and I love them. Every single day is a blessing. The more you know Jesus, the less you need. Jesus is the Christ.

Bibliography

Beecher, Henry Ward. 23 Jan. 2011. 12:12:13 GMT.
    <http://thinkexist.com/quotations/
    forgiveness/>.

Brault, Robert. 12 Oct. 2010. 03:05:36 GMT.
    <http://www.quotegarden.com/god.html>.

Bumper sticker. December 2010. Missoula, Montana.

2 Corinthians 8:9. Lexicon. Biblos.com.

Colvin, Geoff. Talent Is Overrated: What Really Separates World
Class Performers from Everybody Else. New York:
    Portfolio, 2008.

Einstein, Albert. 3 Aug. 2010. 18:40:26 GMT.
    <http://thinkexist.com/quotations/knowledge/>.

Ephesians 6:17. Lexicon. Biblos.com.

Ferraro, Dennis. Phone conversations. April 2010.

Hebrews 4:12-13. Lexicon. Biblos.com.

Herz, Rachel. The Scent of Desire: Discovering Our
    Enigmatic Sense of Smell. New York:
    HarperCollins, 2007. Pgs. ix, 39.

Hufford, Darin. "Who Killed Christ." Weblog entry.
    9 Dec. 2009. Freebelievers Network.

Jackson, J.B. A Dictionary of Scripture Proper Names.
    New Jersey: Loizeaux Brothers, 1987. Pg. 53.

La Fontaine, Jean de. 22 July 2010.
    <http://thinkexist.com/quotations/destiny/   2html>.

Lincoln, Abraham. 13 April 2010. 02:40:43 GMT.
    <http://www.quotations.about.com/cs/inspiration
    quotes/a/power2.htm>.

Matthew 24:23-26. Lexicon. Biblos.com.

Mother Teresa. 23 Nov. 2010. 05:40 PST.
    <http://www.quotegarden.com/prayer.html>.

New International Version Study Bible: 10th Anniversary
    Edition. Ed. Kenneth Barker. Grand Rapids, MI:
    Zondervan Publishing House, 1995.

Proverbs 1:7 & Isaiah 11:2. Lexicon. Biblos.com.

Shore, Zachary. Blunder: Why Smart People Make Bad Decisions. New York: Bloomsbury, 2008. Pg. 32.

Smith, Logan Pearsall. 12 March 2010. 21:00 PST. <http://www.quotegarden.com/money.html>.

Tackett, Denie. Bible study at Corpus Christi. February 2009. Boise, ID.

Tolstoi, Leo Nikolaevich. <http://quotes.libertytree.ca/quotes_about/heresy>.

Wolfe, Thomas. 14 May 2010. 17:56:35 GMT. <http://www.wisdomquotes.com/cat.success.   html>.

www.ingramcontent.com/pod-product-compliance
Lightning Source LLC
Chambersburg PA
CBHW030928090426
42737CB00007B/356